EGYPT

ROBIN GAULDIE

★★★ Highly recommended
★★ Recommended
★ See if you can

This edition is published by Connaught
an imprint of New Holland Publishers Ltd
London • Cape Town • Sydney • Auckland
First published in MCMXCIX
10 9 8 7 6 5 4 3 2 1

website: www.newhollandpublishers.com

Garfield House, 86 Edgware Road
London W2 2EA, United Kingdom

80 McKenzie Street
Cape Town 8001, South Africa

14 Aquatic Drive, Frenchs Forest,
NSW 2086, Australia

218 Lake Road, Northcote,
Auckland, New Zealand

ISBN 1 84517 096 2

Publishing Manager (UK): Simon Pooley
Publishing Manager (SA): Thea Grobbelaar
DTP Cartographic Manager: Genené Hart
Editors: Melany McCallum, Nic Orfang, Thea Grobbelaar, Rowena Curtis, Peter Duncan
Consultant: Neil Hewison
Picture Researcher: Rowena Curtis
Design and DTP: Éloïse Moss
Cartographers: Nicole Engeler, Marlon Christmas, Éloïse Moss

Reproduction by Hirt & Carter (Pty) Ltd, Cape Town
Printed and bound by Times Offset (M) Sdn. Bhd., Malaysia.

Photographic Credits:
Axiom/James Morris: cover (top right, bottom right), title page, pages 7, 8, 9 (top), 10, 12, 14, 17 (top), 19, 25, 28 (top and bottom), 30, 31, 32, 33 (top and bottom), 36, 40, 43, 44, 45, 51, 56, 57, 58 (top and bottom), 60, 65, 68, 71, 73, 74, 76, 78, 82, 83, 87, 89, 92, 94, 95, 96, 97, 99, 106, 107, 110, 112 (top), 116, 118, 119, 120;
Axiom/Dorian Shaw: pages 54, 63, 64;
Robin Gauldie: pages 15, 20, 27, 80, 86;
Life File/Graham Buchan: page 6;
Life File/Maggie Fagan: pages 84, 108;
Life File/Barry Mayes: pages 22, 26, 105;
Life File/Terry O'Brien: pages 17 (bottom), 88;
Life File/Amanda Talbot: page 9 (bottom);
Life File/Sue Wheat: pages 24, 61, 62;
Mary Evans Picture Library: pages 18, 21, 23;
James Morris: pages 4, 13, 34, 42, 72, 98, 111;
The Ancient Egypt Picture Library: page 59;
PhotoBank/Jeanetta Baker: page 100;
PhotoBank/ Peter Baker: cover (top left), pages 16, 39, 79, 85;
Mariëlle Renssen: cover (bottom left), pages 47, 48, 49, 50;
Lawson Wood: pages 11 (top and bottom), 29, 35, 102, 109, 112 (bottom), 113.

Cover Photographs
Top left: *Tutankhamun, perhaps the most famous Pharaoh of all.*
Top right: *A palm tree-lined canal at Luxor.*
Bottom left: *The pyramids at Giza.*
Bottom right: *Sunset on the Nile River.*

Title page: *Fishing with a net on the Nile near Aswan.*

CONTENTS

1
Introducing Egypt

There is no country in the world quite like Egypt. The awe-inspiring relics of the world's mightiest ancient civilization have drawn countless visitors here since the earliest times to marvel at the breathtaking works of the **Pharaohs**, from the massive stone hulks of the pyramids to the graceful columns and stern colossi of **Karnak** and **Abu Simbel**. The speculation caused by these magnificent buildings persists even today. Later civilizations frequently asked themselves whether such wonders could really be the work of mere mortals, or whether they were in fact inspired by supernatural or superhuman beings.

Yet the antiquities of Egypt, wonderful as they are, are only a small part of this huge land's unique appeal. Part of the Arab world yet not wholly of it, Egypt looks south across the Nubian Desert to the heart of Africa and north across the Mediterranean Sea to Europe. The country is a culture shaped by many influences. Most of its people live, as they have always lived, within a few hundred metres of the life-giving **Nile River**, yet a handful of stubborn nomads still haunt the empty spaces of the **Sinai Peninsula** and the **Western Desert**. Millions of people dwell in the great urban sprawl of **Cairo**, one of the world's largest cities, yet a few score kilometres outside this throbbing metropolis are delta villages where rural life has changed very little in centuries, while a day's drive away in the empty Western Desert are oasis settlements that rarely see a visitor from the outside world.

Top Attractions

*** **Pyramids and Sphinx:** the symbols of ancient Egypt.
*** **Temple of Karnak:** giant columns and statues.
*** **Luxor West Bank and Valley of the Kings:** tombs and temples along the Nile.
*** **Abu Simbel:** legendary rescued temples and colossi.
** **Mount Sinai and the Monastery of St Catherine:** Christian site in the desert.
** **Egyptian Antiquities Museum in Cairo:** treasures from the Pharaohs' tombs.
** **Red Sea dive sites:** clear waters, colourful marine life.

Opposite: *Feluccas with their triangular sails are a common sight on the Nile.*

Right: *The Nile provides sharp scenic contrasts between arid mountains and lush green farmland.*

Statistics

Official name: The Arab Republic of Egypt.
Area: 1,001,450 sq km (386,660 sq miles).
Population (estimated): 69 million.
Population growth: 1.99 per cent in 2002.
Infant mortality: 44 per 1000 (down from 81 per 1000 in 1981).
Capital: Cairo, population estimated at 15–20 million.
Second city: Alexandria, population 5 million.
Highest mountain: Mt St Catherine (Jebel Katerina), 2637m (8651ft).
Longest river: Nile, about 6690km (4160 miles) from source to mouth, 940km (584 miles) crossing Egypt.
Official language: Arabic.
Official religion: Islam.
Currency: The Egyptian pound (E£).

THE LAND

Egypt is shaped by the **Nile**. Swollen by the rains of the East African highlands, the world's longest river (about 6690km [4160 miles] long) deposited vast quantities of fertile soil along its banks and in the richly fertile delta region, making farming possible in a desert country that, except along the Mediterranean coast, receives virtually no rainfall. Until 1971, with the completion of the huge High Dam at Aswan, the Nile flooded once a year along its entire length. The extent of the flood could spell prosperity or disaster for millions. Now, the waters of the Nile have been pent up to form **Lake Nasser**, a vast man-made reservoir that not only provides a steady flow of water year-round but also supplies the entire country with hydro-electric power.

Almost all of Egypt's territory is desert, and the contrast between the vivid green of the irrigated farmland along the Nile and the leafless aridity of the desert only a few metres away is one of the most enduring memories of every traveller. Efforts are being made to direct Nile water to desert areas – most notably a rather grandiose project to lead water from Lake Nasser to the Tushka area of the Nubian Desert – but whether Egypt can succeed in making the desert bloom is yet to be seen.

Modern Egypt's southern border, with **Sudan**, and its western border, with **Libya**, are arbitrary lines drawn in the desert sand by former colonial rulers in 1956. North of Cairo, the Nile divides into two channels which form the Delta and empty into the **Mediterranean** along a stretch of coastline 200km (124 miles) long. The Nile Delta (Lower Egypt) comprises hundreds of thousands of square kilometres of lush farmland, home to 30 million people – 44 per cent of the country's total population.

On the western edge of the Nile Delta is **Alexandria**, the country's second-largest city and its major seaport. Not far beyond the eastern limit of the Delta, the Suez Canal cuts across the Isthmus of Suez, separating western Egypt from the **Sinai Peninsula**, and technically separating the continents of Africa and Asia. Bounded

HARD CURRENCY

Cotton is Egypt's main export crop. **Oil** and **natural gas** from offshore wells in the Gulf of Suez and onshore operations in Sinai account for about half the country's exports. **Tolls** from ships using the Suez Canal are another huge foreign currency earner, as is **tourism**. **Industrial production**, concentrated around Cairo and Alexandria, includes phosphates, manganese, iron, steel, aluminium, and coal.

Below: *Massive crescent dunes dominate the almost lifeless sand sea of the Western Desert.*

Above: *The rugged mountains of Sinai, backdrop to the story of Moses and the search for the Biblical promised land.*

in the north by the Mediterranean, in the west by the Canal and the Gulf of Suez and in the east by the Gulf of Aqaba, Sinai is a region of arid, mountainous desert, with a string of small holiday resorts situated along its east coast. Egypt's frontier with Israel cuts right across Sinai from the Mediterranean to the foot of the Gulf of Aqaba, close to the popular Israeli resort of Eilat and the Jordanian seaport, Aqaba.

South of Suez, Egypt's Red Sea coast is separated from the settled farmland of the Nile Valley by the **Eastern Desert**. There are not very many settlements along this inhospitable coastline, though **Hurghada**, situated close to the mouth of the Gulf of Suez, has developed into a holiday resort popular with divers and with European holiday-makers seeking winter sunshine and sandy beaches.

South of Cairo, the Nile Valley is traditionally known as **Upper Egypt**, with settlements strung out at intervals along the Nile for almost 1000km (621 miles) until settlement comes to an abrupt halt at Aswan, where the **Nubian Desert** begins.

Egypt's main highway runs from Alexandria, on the coast, through the Delta to Cairo and the length of the Nile Valley via Luxor as far as Aswan. Other main roads run from Cairo down to Suez and along the Red Sea coast to Hurghada and points south; across the Eastern Desert between Hurghada and Qena on the Nile; and a loop route has recently been opened connecting the oases of the Western Desert with Cairo. A railway runs parallel to the main highway from the coast to Aswan.

THE PLAGUES OF EGYPT

Is there a scientific basis for the story of the Biblical plagues called down by Moses to force the release of the enslaved Israelites? At least two of the plagues – the turning of the Nile into blood and the plague of frogs – could have been the result of a 'red tide' of the algae *pfisteria*, which releases a neurotoxin fatal to fish. With no fish to prey on tadpoles, the frog population could have exploded. Also, fungal mycotoxins infecting stored grain could have caused the Biblical 'death of the firstborn'.

Plants of the Ancient World

The **papyrus reed**, used by the early Egyptians to make the world's first paper, no longer grows abundantly along the Nile, though it can be seen in botanical gardens, such as those on Kitchener's Island at Aswan. The **lotus flower** was sacred to the Pharaohs and is a common element in paintings and statuary, often carved into column capitals. The lotus still flowers in the marshy Nile Delta region.

Climate

Most visitors find the winter months, from November to March, the best time to visit. Cairo, Luxor and the Nile Valley are generally sunny and warm at this time of year, with daytime temperatures around 20–24°C (68–75°F). At night, temperatures can fall as low as 5°C (41°F). Hurghada, Sharm el-Sheikh, and the other Red Sea resorts can have daytime temperatures of up to 30°C (86°F) at this time of year, though even here night-time temperatures can drop sharply. Except along the Mediterranean coast, where northern gales can bring wet weather in winter, rain is a rarity at any time of year.

Temperatures start to rise in May. Cairo, the Red Sea coast, and Upper Egypt can become extremely hot, with temperatures capable of reaching 35–40°C (95–104°F). At this time of year, many of the wealthier Cairenes traditionally desert the stifling conditions of the capital for the somewhat more pleasant climate of the Mediterranean coast. Committed sun-worshippers (or divers who intend to spend most of the day underwater) may find the beach resorts tolerable at this time of year, but if your main reason for going to Egypt is to see the sights of Cairo, Luxor and the Nile Valley, it would be unproductive to go in high summer.

Above: *Ox-power is still used to raise water for irrigation in many places.*
Below: *Irrigation canals lead water from the Nile to the farmlands on the banks.*

Cats

Archaeological evidence shows that cats had come to be worshipped as gods in Egypt (along with a divine menagerie of other creatures that included the hawk, the ibis, the cow, the hippo, the crocodile, the cobra and the dung-beetle) by 2800BC. When a cat died, its owner shaved his eyebrows as a token of both mourning and respect, and cats were routinely mummified and buried with great ceremony. So many were mummified that in the later Middle Ages their bodies were shipped to Europe by the ton to be used as fertilizer.

Flora and Fauna

At first glance, Egypt has relatively few niches for wildlife. The Nile Valley, settled and intensively cultivated for millennia, is an almost entirely domesticated environment, while the barren desert beyond is habitable only by a few specialized species, such as the desert fox, the desert rat, the wild ass and the Egyptian gazelle. Hippopotamus, depicted in ancient frescoes as dwelling in the Egyptian Nile, have long been extinct, as are lion and leopard, which reputedly lived in the Egyptian desert as recently as 2000 years ago. Crocodiles, also seen in frescoes, are rare but have been sighted in recent years in Lake Nasser south of Aswan. Snakes, once a symbol of the Pharaohs, are rarely seen.

That said, **bird life** is abundant in the Delta. The salt marshes and brackish lakes near the coast attract huge flocks of migrating waterfowl. White **herons** and cattle **egrets** can be seen wading in the flooded fields or nesting in the trees along the Nile or irrigation canals. Pied **kingfishers** hover above the river, plunging to catch small fish, tadpoles or water insects, and white and black **storks** can be seen on migration. Red kites soar and kestrels hover, even in the skies of Cairo. There are several species of **vulture**, most commonly the Egyptian vulture, easily distinguished by its all-white plumage. Visitors may also be lucky enough to see more colourful species such as the **Nile Valley sunbird** and **golden oriole** and, in the less-degraded of the brackish coastal lakes, spectacular water birds such as the **greater flamingo**, **Mediterranean pelican**, and **Egyptian goose**. The hoopoe, with its striking crest, is often seen along the roadsides.

Few wild **mammals** can find sufficient space to live in the small areas

Below: *Bird life is quite bountiful around water sources such as the lakes of the Dakhla Oasis.*

of cultivation, but several species of **bat** are common. **Jackals** live on the fringes of cultivated land and have also been known to raid garbage tips. Although they are becoming increasingly rare, flocks of **desert gazelle** and herds of **wild ass** still survive in the Eastern Desert and the Sinai Peninsula. Domesticated **camels** are the Bedouin's favoured form of transport, though as often as not they carry tourists rather than caravan goods. For the peasant villagers of the Nile and the Delta, the **donkey** and the **mule** are still essential.

A far richer abundance of life can be seen in the depths of Egypt's seas. The beautiful reefs of the Red Sea are famed among divers worldwide for the wealth and variety of their stunning **marine life**, which ranges from tiny invertebrates and brilliantly coloured soft corals to sharks, rays, grouper and moray eel.

The **date palm**, which is almost synonymous with Egypt, grows all over the place, especially in gardens and courtyards. In the oases of the Western Desert, thousands of date palms provide the population's staple diet.

Above: *Camels are more often used to carry tourists than to transport cargo.*
Below: *Masked butterfly-fish are one of many species to be seen on Egypt's reefs.*

ARAB HORSES

It is claimed that the horses pictured in Egyptian inscriptions dating from as long ago as 1400BC are the ancestors of the horses now known as Arab. The best place to see them in Egypt today is at **Al-Zahraa Farm**, 20km (12 miles) from central Cairo in the village of Kafr Gamos, where more than 250 mares and 130 stallions are kept. The farm was founded by Mohammed Ali Pasha and since then has been the focus of horse breeding in Egypt, employing 2000 people and earning some US$1.5 million annually from the sale of Arab thoroughbreds, notably those of the El-Sakalawy, El-Kohylan, El-Abyan and El-Habdan bloodlines.

HISTORY IN BRIEF

The history of the Nile civilizations stretches so far back into the dawn of time that it is almost impossible to grasp. Egypt makes the era of the Greek city states or the Roman Empire seem like yesterday and, unlike ancient Greece or Rome, the empire of the Pharaohs left little literature or written history to allow us a glimpse into its life.

The Archaic Period

Stone tools discovered at several archaeological sites in the Nile Valley indicate that there were tool-using Neolithic communities in Egypt as early as 6000–7000BC. By around 3300BC these communities began to be drawn together under one ruler, and at some point between 3200 and 3000BC the first strong ruler of the Nile Valley,

HISTORICAL CALENDAR

3000–341BC Pharaonic Era.
332–30BC Ptolemaic (Greek or Hellenistic) Era.
30BC–AD638 The Roman/ Byzantine Era.
640–1517 Arab Conquest and Mameluke Rule.
1517–1882 Ottoman Conquest and Rule.
1798–1801 French Invasion.
1805–48 Mohammed Ali rules as Pasha or Wali (viceroy), succeeded in 1848 by his son Ibrahim, then after Ibrahim's death by his grandson, Abbas.
1848–54 Abbas rules as Pasha, described by historians as 'harsh but capable'.
1854–63 Reign of Said Pasha.
1863–79 Ismail, eldest surviving son of Ibrahim, rules first as Pasha, then from 1869 as Khedive (with greater autonomy from the Sultan in Constantinople).
1879–92 Ismail's eldest son Tawfiq succeeds after Ismail deposed by Sultan under pressure from France and Britain
1882 Egyptian army mutinies. Officers led by Arabi Pasha fortify Alexandria which is attacked by British fleet. Arabi defeated at Tel el-Kebir by British troops. British occupy Cairo.
1882–1952 British Occupation and Protectorate.
1892–1922 Abbas Hilmi, son of Tawfiq, succeeds on his father's death.
1922 Nominal independence from Britain.
1922–36 Fuad 1 succeeds Abbas Hilmi as the first king of Egypt.
1936–52 Reign of King Farouk. Egypt nominally independent, but Farouk seen as British puppet.
1939–45 World War II.
1948 Involvement in first Arab–Israeli War.
1952 Overthrow of King Farouk.
1953 Declaration of Republic in June.
1954–70 Gamal Abdel Nasser's term as President.
1956 Suez Crisis: French, British and Israeli troops invade Suez Canal zone in October/ November; US ultimatum forces withdrawal.
1967 Six Day War with Israel (5–11 June), loss of Sinai.
1970–81 Anwar Sadat's term as President.
1973 October War with Israel, failure to regain Sinai.
1979 Peace with Israel under Camp David agreement.
1981 Sadat assassinated by Islamic Jihad terrorists, 6 October.
1982 Return of occupied Sinai.
1981 Hosni Mubarak becomes President of Egypt.
1998 Restoration of Sphinx completed. Egyptian scientists discover lost capital of Ramses II at Qantir in the Nile Delta.

Menes, founded the first of the 30 dynasties that were destined to rule Egypt for almost three millennia.

Menes and the two dynasties which succeeded him ruled for four centuries, with their capital at Memphis, just south of present-day Cairo. During this time they unified Lower and Upper Egypt and created, from a patchwork of valley tribes, the world's first great empire.

The Old Kingdom

Between 2686 and 2181BC the 3rd and 4th Dynasties ruled Egypt. Their capital, too, was at Memphis, but they began to built vast tombs, temples and pyramids at Saqqara, Giza, Abousir and Dahshur. The empire's political and social structures evolved, becoming both more complex and more stable, with the semi-divine **Pharaoh** at the apex, wielding absolute temporal, military and religious power and making his will felt through a sophisticated civil service.

This high degree of organization, coupled with the fertility and climatic stability of the Nile Valley, gave the Old Kingdom the ability to use its surplus labour to build the monumental works that we today associate most strongly with ancient Egypt: the great pyramids of Cheops, Chephren and Mycerinus at Giza, erected during the 4th Dynasty. Religious doctrine was now codified into an extremely complex theology based on the sun, with a pantheon of deities concerned with every aspect of life and death.

Now, too, Egypt began to look beyond its early borders, sending trading ships to Punt (present-day Somalia) for gold, slaves and ivory, and to the Arabian Peninsula for timber and aromatic resins. Copper and turquoise began to be mined in Sinai, and on the southern frontier the Egyptians began to exploit the gold mines of Nubia.

OSIRIS AND ISIS

Osiris, lord of the underworld, is depicted both seated and standing. Like Amun, he carries the flail and crook of kingship and his conical crown has ram's horns. Osiris was said to have taught the Egyptians cultivation, and ruled with his bride and sister, Isis, who bore him a son, the hawk-headed god Horus. Osiris was murdered by his jealous brother Seth, who chopped his body into 14 parts which he threw into the Nile. Isis hunted for each part, and buried each where she found it, which is why there were so many Osiris temples along the Nile.

Opposite: *Relics of the Old Kingdom, seen today in the Egyptian Antiquities Museum in Cairo.*
Below: *The Alabaster Sphinx at Memphis is better preserved than its famous relative at Giza.*

MUMMIFICATION

The Egyptians believed in an eternal life after death, but they also believed that the endurance of the *ka*, or spirit, was linked to the preservation of the body, hence their obsession with mummification, which was an exact science. Mummification took about two months, and was begun by removing the brain (through the nose) and the intestines, liver, stomach and lungs, which were treated and kept in separate containers called Canopic jars. The heart, believed to be the seat of the mind and soul, was left in place, as were the kidneys. The body was filled and covered with natron, a dehydrating agent, for five weeks, before removing the packing and stuffing it with clay, resin, sawdust and perfumes. The final stage was to coat it with resin and fragrant unguents, wrap it in bandages and place it in its decorated sarcophagus.

First Intermediate Period

The end of the Old Kingdom is marked by the collapse of the central power of Memphis between 2200 and 2050BC, probably due to the increasing power of the provincial governors, who first revolted against the throne, then fought amongst themselves, while the weakened monarchs of the 7th and 8th Dynasties were powerless to re-establish control. This period of anarchy is known as the First Intermediate Period and is generally dated 2181–2040BC.

The Middle Kingdom

Certain of the warring princes then began to consolidate their power and acquire royal ambitions. Between 2160 and 2040BC the Pharaohs of the 9th and 10th Dynasties established monarchic rule based at Heracleopolis, near modern Asyut, only to be overthrown by the **Theban kings** of the 11th Dynasty. This Middle Kingdom spans the period of 2040–1782BC, with its capital initially at Thebes (Luxor). During the 11th and 12th Dynasties, the capital was moved north again, to Lisht. This was a time of reform, consolidation and expansion. Laws were passed to encourage farmers, and as a result the fertile El-Faiyum region became one of the wealthiest parts of Egypt. But Egypt expanded, too, advancing south to conquer Nubia, and becoming a commercial power the length of the Red Sea and far into the Middle East. Abydos, in Upper Egypt, flowered into a major religious centre with the rise of the cult of **Osiris**.

Below: *Hippopotamus were among the sacred animals of ancient Egypt.*

Second Intermediate Period

Between 1782 and 1570BC Egypt once again plunged into disorder. The cause this time was an invasion from abroad. The Hyksos, a warlike nation from Asia Minor, rolled across Palestine and Sinai, then into Egypt, where their conquests were aided by their mastery of the horse and the chariot – neither of which were in use in Egypt – and by sophisticated bronze tools and weapons.

The **Hyksos** settled first in the fertile Nile Delta where they built their capital, Avaris. They then pushed to the south along the Nile Valley. Meanwhile, on Egypt's southern frontier, part of Nubia was lost to rebellious local rulers. The Theban princes of the 17th Dynasty fought back bravely against the encroaching Hyksos, who were eventually driven out of Egyptian territory under **Ahmose**, founder of the 18th Dynasty, whose reign ushered in the era of the New Kingdom.

Above: *A statue of Tuthmosis, one of many at the Temple of Hatshepsut near Luxor.*

The New Kingdom

This was the time of Egypt's greatest power, with the rule of the Pharaohs stretching from the fourth cataract of the Nile (in the Sudan) to the Euphrates River (in what is now Iraq in southwest Asia). The impressive feats of the 18th Dynasty rulers are recorded in detail in hieroglyphs such as those that can be seen at the Karnak temple complex near Luxor. **Hatshepsut** (1498–1483BC), the first woman to rule Egypt as queen in her own right, ordered the building of magnificent temples and monuments, many of which were subsequently vandalized by her successor, **Tuthmosis III**. Tuthmosis's own buildings and inscriptions secure his place as Egypt's greatest military leader, recording an impressive 17 campaigns against the Hittite kings of Asia Minor and the Mitanni (or Medes) of the Euphrates Valley. Tuthmosis III's conquests were followed by a period of consolidation, peace, and intermarriage between the Egyptian royal family and members of the Hittite and Mitanni ruling families. This era of peace and prosperity represents the apogee of Egypt under the Pharaohs. It allowed the country's rulers to transfer their attention from conquest and domination to religion and monumental projects designed to perpetuate their names for posterity and

Ra and Other Sun Gods

The Egyptians worshipped the sun in many guises. Ra is pictured as a man with a falcon's head, crowned with the holy disc of the Sun. He crossed the sky in his solar boat, rising from the world below in the east and setting in the west, which the Egyptians associated with the land of the dead. Ra had many identities, including Khepri, the sacred scarab which brings the rising sun, and eventually became merged with Amun as the most important of the ancient deities. Aten or Aton was another aspect of Ra, as was Atum, the setting sun.

ensure the favour of their many gods. Amenophis III (1386–1349BC) built the magnificent Temple of Luxor which still stands, as well as a much larger temple on the west bank of the Nile of which all that remains are the two huge statues known as the Colossi of Memnon.

Amenophis's successor, **Akhnaten**, veered away from the orthodox pantheon and its most important deity, Amun. Instead, he decreed the cult of Aten, depicted as a solar disc. He moved his capital from Thebes to Akhetaten, near modern Tell el-Amarna. Once again, an absorption with internal affairs inevitably led to disintegration at the empire's fringes, and parts of Egypt's eastern conquests were lost to rebellious local rulers or to the rival Hittite Empire. Akhnaten's religion died with him, but two fortuitous archaeological finds have ensured his place in Egypt's history. The first is the bust of his Queen, **Nefertiti**, whose name became synonymous with female beauty. The second was the discovery of the tomb of his son and heir, **Tutankhamun**, who restored the old religion. He reigned for only seven years, dying at the age of 19 and bringing the royal line of the 18th Dynasty to an end.

Seti I (1302–1290BC), the second Pharaoh of the 19th Dynasty, set about restoring the ways of the Old Kingdom, and his successor **Ramses II** (1290–1224BC) built some of the most striking of the monuments which survive today, including the temple of the Ramesseum on the west bank at Luxor, and also the magnificent colossi of Abu Simbel. Ramses also curbed the threat from the east, defeating the Hittites at the Battle of Kadesh. **Merneptah**, Ramses II's successor, defeated a Libyan invasion of the Delta region.

Death on the Nile

Was Tutankhamun really murdered? He was, some writers argue, the puppet of a priesthood keen to reclaim power after being sidelined by his father-in-law and predecessor, Akhnaten. After Tutankhamun's death, the high priest Ay ruled Egypt until his death four years later. But is there any evidence that Ay had the boy king murdered? X-rays of the mummy showed a thickening at the base of the skull that might (or might not) have been a blow. The theories are entertaining – but there is nothing to convince a jury.

Decline of the Pharaohs

With the onset of the 20th Dynasty under **Ramses III** in 1195BC, the long decline of the Pharaohs begins. Ramses III is best known for his victories over the Sea Peoples (who were probably Achaean Greeks from the Aegean and Eastern Mediterranean) and the Libyans. Yet the very reliefs which record his victories portray an empire under assault from all sides. Attackers from outside found Egypt divided by a power struggle between the Pharaohs and the hereditary high priests of Amun.

Between the end of the 20th Dynasty in 1090BC and the advent of Alexander in 332BC, few dynasties lasted more than 150 years and the centre of power shifted from the Delta to Upper Egypt and back again. A Libyan dynasty ruling from Tanis gave way to Nubian kings who conquered Upper Egypt, then the whole empire, only for their capital at Thebes to be pillaged by Assyrian invaders. Sais in the Delta became the centre of power in the 7th and 6th centuries BC and its rulers called in Greek mercenaries to drive out the Assyrians.

Egypt was attached to the Persian Empire throughout the 5th century BC, and Greek help was called in again to expel them at the beginning of the 4th century BC. The Persians returned in 343BC, only to be conquered in their turn by **Alexander the Great** in 332BC. After the wars of succession which followed Alexander's death and the collapse of his short-lived empire, his most brilliant general crowned himself **Ptolemy I Soter**.

Art

Ancient Egyptian sculptors worked in materials including marble, limestone, pink and black granite, soapstone and alabaster as well as wood and precious metals. Their colours came from chalk, red carnelian, turquoise, yellow jasper and black diorite and have proved amazingly durable. Painting on the walls of tombs and temples is highly stylized, with the heads of figures, but not their eyes or shoulders, shown in profile.

Opposite: *The face of Tutankhamun, perhaps the most famous Pharaoh of all.*
Above: *Model soldiers accompanied the mummified body of the Pharaoh.*
Below: *The head of Ramses II at the Ramesseum has suffered at the hands of vandals over the centuries.*

Greek Genius

The Hellenistic Greeks of Alexandria under the Ptolemies were the most inventive technologists of their time. A large part of their work was lost with the destruction of the Great Library of Alexandria, but from much-copied fragments of military and civil engineering texts of the past, we know of some of their more impressive inventions: one **Dionysus** of Alexandria invented the *polybolos*, a tripod-mounted, multi-shot crossbow for repelling pirates. His contemporary, **Hero**, invented a pump for firefighting, an air-powered organ, and even a jet-propulsion steam engine. Meanwhile, Alexandrian shipwrights were building the greatest warships the world had yet seen. **Callixenus** of Rhodes, a writer from the 3rd century BC, describes a gigantic trireme, 140m (459ft) long and with a crew of 4000 oarsmen and 2850 marines.

The Ptolemies

From their capital at Alexandria, the Ptolemaic kings made Egypt part of the Hellenic Mediterranean world. They in turn were influenced by the culture of Egypt. In Alexandria, they built the famed Library and the Pharos (lighthouse), one of the Seven Wonders of the ancient world listed by the traveller and historian Herodotus. In addition, Ptolemy III extended the Karnak temple complex and began building the temple at Edfu; to Ptolemy IV we owe the temples at Esna and Kom Ombo; and Ptolemy XII built temples at Dendera, Edfu and Philae.

The Romans

By the 1st century AD the rising tide of Roman power was lapping at Egypt's frontiers. Ptolemy XII held the Romans off by diplomacy. His successor, **Cleopatra VII**, tried to avoid conquest by alliance and dalliance, first with Julius Caesar, then with Mark Anthony. Caesar's assassination was followed by civil war, first between his followers and the assassins, then between Octavian, Caesar's adopted nephew, and his former ally Mark Anthony. Octavian defeated the combined forces of Anthony and Cleopatra at Actium, off the Greek coast, and seized Alexandria in 30BC. Anthony and Cleopatra committed suicide, and Egypt was added to the Roman Empire, remaining a Roman province for the next seven centuries. Christianity was introduced by St Mark in

Right: *Cleopatra reclining in a carriage, surrounded by her attendants.*
Opposite: *The stately columns of the Roman basilica at El-Ashmunein, formerly known as Hermopolis Magna.*

AD45, but with the partition of the Empire into eastern and western empires in AD379, Egypt came under the rule of **Constantinople,** the capital of the eastern Roman Empire (Byzantium).

The Coming of Islam

Egypt was protected by distance from the barbarian invasions from east and north which toppled the Western Roman Empire in AD476. It was distanced too from the permanent state of war on Byzantium's other borders. The coming of Islam was rapid and unexpected. In AD640 – only 18 years after the beginning of the Islamic calendar – the banners of the militant new faith swept into Egypt on the lances of Arab horsemen. Cairo fell to the Arabs in 641, Alexandria in 642. For the next two centuries, the Muslim Emirs of Egypt were vassals of the Abbassid Caliphate of **Baghdad**, then the capital of the Islamic world. In 878 Ibn Tulun, governor of Egypt, set himself up as independent ruler of Egypt. On his death, however, the Caliphate regained control of Egypt, which was ruled by vassals of Baghdad until 969, when it was conquered by the Fatimid Caliphs of Kairouan. The early Fatimid Caliphs moved their capital from Tunisia to the Nile, founding a new city appropriately named El-Qahira (the victorious). **Cairo** quickly became one of the most important political, religious and cultural centres of the Islamic world.

The Great Library

The Arab conquerors of the 7th century AD are often blamed for the sack of the Great Library at Alexandria, created under the Ptolemies and at one time the greatest storehouse of knowledge in the world. Alexandria was sacked and burned by the Arabs in 646, but by then most of the library's manuscripts had already been destroyed – by Christian bishops who anathematized their secular learning and their pagan philosophy, or by monks who recycled the precious parchments and used them to write Christian texts. The Arab rulers, by contrast, were great patrons of learning and the arts.

The Age of Saladin

In the year 1079, the Western European knights of the First Crusade landed in Palestine with the intention of driving the Muslims out of the Holy Land and recapturing

Jerusalem for Christendom. The **Crusaders** set up a chain of petty kingdoms and duchies along the Mediterranean coast. With the help of reinforcements from Europe, they expanded steadily, capturing Jerusalem in 1099. By the mid-12th century they threatened Egypt, but their decisive defeat by the Kurdish Muslim leader Salah el-Din (Saladin) turned the tide against them. Jerusalem was recaptured in 1187 and the Crusader kingdoms were completely reconquered. **Saladin** went on to make himself ruler of Egypt, fortifying Cairo and building the massive Citadel which still stands in the heart of the old city.

The Mamelukes

Saladin's heirs ruled until the year 1250 when the throne passed by marriage to Aybak, chief of the Mamelukes. This elite corps of soldier-slaves now became the most powerful political and military class in Egypt, and Mameluke Sultans ruled from Cairo over the next three centuries. Their rule was harsh, often corrupt and marked by treachery and deceit.

SALADIN

Salah el-Din Yusuf ibn Ayyub was not an Arab but a Muslim Kurd. Commanding the army of the Emir (king) of Syria, Nur el-Din, he helped conquer Egypt, later making himself viceroy under the Caliph of Baghdad, who confirmed him as Sultan of Egypt and Syria in 1174. After conquering Mesopotamia (modern Iraq), he attacked the Crusader kingdoms of the Holy Land, inflicting a crippling defeat on them at Hattin in 1187. The Third Crusade, led by Richard I (Lionheart) of England, checked his expansion and forced him to yield the Mediterranean coast cities and allow Christian pilgrims to enter Jerusalem. The Crusaders regarded Saladin as their worthiest and most honourable foe, and his dynasty ruled Egypt until it was overthrown by the Mamelukes in 1250.

The Ottoman Empire

Meanwhile, the Ottoman Turks who had first emerged from Central Asia around the 9th century AD had completed their conquest of Asia Minor. The Ottomans rolled back the frontiers of the **Byzantine Empire**, finally conquering Constantinople itself in 1453. In 1517 Sultan **Suleiman the Magnificent** turned his attention to Egypt, meeting no effective opposition from the Mamelukes, who proved incapable of uniting to resist the Turks. For the next three centuries, Egypt remained part of an Ottoman Empire which stretched from the Balkans to the Red Sea, and was ruled by a series of governors (Pashas) appointed by the Sultan in Constantinople. Egypt became a backwater of empire, though the Islamic university of El-Azhar, founded in 971, continued to be the greatest theological centre of the entire Muslim world.

The French

The outside world impinged violently on Egypt once again with the landing in 1798 of a French Revolutionary expeditionary force led by Napoleon Bonaparte. Napoleon's aim was to bring Egypt within the French sphere of influence, allowing him to control the important trade route to India via the Isthmus of Suez and the Red Sea. But the expedition was more than just a military adventure. Napoleon brought with him some of France's finest scholars, eager to study the treasures of the ancient world. His soldiers may have carved their names into the stones of temples and obelisks (where they are to this day), but the scientists and archaeologists who accompanied them began the rediscovery of ancient Egypt. The deciphering of the hieroglyphic script, for example, owes almost everything to the expedition's discovery of the **Rosetta Stone** in 1799.

Napoleon's expedition, however, was destined for disaster. While the French land forces were engaged in seizing the capital, Admiral Horatio Nelson's ships sank the French fleet which was anchored at Aboukir Bay, cutting the expeditionary force off from supplies and reinforcement. Napoleon himself slipped back to France and in 1801 the remnants of his expeditionary force also withdrew.

Ottoman Rank

The emperor in Constantinople was known in the West as the **Sultan** (a secular title) but to his subjects he was also the **Caliph**, or supreme ruler of all Islam in line of succession from Mohammed. Below him was a complex system of ranks. The rulers of 19th-century Egypt became **Khedives** – a dynasty of virtually independent kings who paid token tribute to the Sultan. They had previously been mere **Walis** (viceroys) or **Pashas** (provincial military governors). Lower regional governors, sometimes hereditary chieftains, were known as **Beys**.

Opposite: *Minarets like this one at Luxor dominate the skylines of virtually every Egyptian town.*
Below: *Napoleon confronts the Sphinx, then almost buried in sand.*

MOHAMMED ALI

Mohammed (or Mehmet) Ali was born in the Greek port of Kavala (then, like Egypt, part of the Ottoman Empire), and came to Egypt as an officer in the Turkish army. In 1811 he ended the power of the Mamelukes by a ruthless massacre of their leaders. From 1813–18 his son, Ibrahim, campaigned against the Wahabi zealots of Arabia, recapturing the holy cities of Medina and Mecca for the Sultan. Mohammed then set Ibrahim to create a modern army to campaign for the Ottoman Sultan against Greek rebels. After the war, Mohammed demanded greater independence from the Sultan. When this was refused, he rebelled, driving the Turkish troops out of Palestine and Syria and gaining control of large parts of Turkey itself. This meteoric success of his was too much for the great powers of Europe, who forced him to give up his conquests. He abdicated in 1848.

Mohammed Ali Pasha

The French episode had destroyed the Ottoman hold on Egypt and encouraged a new generation of Egyptians to seek change. From the chaos that followed the French withdrawal emerged a new leader, an officer of Greek-Albanian birth named **Mohammed Ali**. With the support of the army, he declared himself Pasha of Egypt. In theory, he recognized the Sultan in Constantinople as his overlord. In practice, he controlled Egypt as an independent ruler for the next 40 years, during which time he imposed a programme of modernization aimed at dragging the country out of the Middle Ages. Egypt was to be a forgotten backwater no longer, and Mohammed Ali's successors, ruling with the title of Khedive, abandoned any pretence of being vassals of the Ottoman Empire.

The Co-Dominium

With the expansion of European empires in Asia, interest increased in creating a faster route via the Isthmus of Suez as an alternative to the long and arduous journey around the Cape of Good Hope. The visionary French engineer Ferdinand de Lesseps inspired the building of the **Suez Canal**, which opened in 1869 to great acclaim. Egypt initially held 44 per cent of the shares in the international fund which financed the canal, but the Khedive Ismail's financial incompetence forced him to sell out to British and French financiers. In 1876, a Franco-British

Right: *The Mosque of Mohammed Ali was founded by Egypt's greatest 19th-century figure.*
Opposite: *The Suez Canal was the most astounding engineering achievement of the 19th century.*

Napoleon's Savants

The French invasion of 1798 reopened European eyes to Egypt. In the spirit of scientific-minded revolutionary France, Napoleon brought along 167 scientists of all disciplines, their mission to provide a comprehensive analysis of ancient and contemporary Egypt. It took 15 years for the information they gathered to be collated and printed as the 24-volume *Description d'Egypte*. With its vivid illustrations by the group's artists, it kindled a new fascination with the country and inspired generations of travellers.

'co-dominium' was set up to manage the Khedive's affairs, and in 1882 Britain sent a garrison to Alexandria. The intense imperial rivalry between Britain and France, and the need to control the vital Canal route, encouraged Britain to tighten its grip on Egypt, which became little more than a British protectorate with the Khedive a British puppet.

The large British and French presence in the country generated a lot of interest in the relics of the Pharaohs, and systematic uncovering of the tombs and temples of Giza, Memphis, Luxor and other archaeological sites now began. At first this was little more than organized tomb-looting by adventurers who were more interested in the fantastic treasures to be found within than in real archaeology. The founding of the Institute of Archaeology in 1880 helped to bring about a more scientific approach.

Egypt formally became a British protectorate in 1914, but then in 1922 it regained its independence, though Britain kept control of defence and of the Suez Canal.

Sa'ad Zaghloul

Sa'ad Zaghloul (1860–1927), after whom many Egyptian city streets and squares are named, became minister for education in 1907 and rose to lead the **Wafd nationalist movement**. On 13 November 1918, at the conclusion of World War I, he demanded the abolition of the British protectorate and full independence for Egypt, which was refused. Zaghloul's resignation triggered riots, and he was arrested and exiled with his leading supporters to Malta. He returned to Egypt only to be exiled again from 1921–23, and was elected **prime minister** by a landslide in the first Egyptian elections in 1924. He died in 1927.

World War II

During World War II the Suez Canal was strategically absolutely vital and there was heavy fighting in the Western Desert, first between Italian and Allied forces, then, after the defeat of the Italians, between the Allies and the German army under Erwin Rommel. In November 1942 the decisive Allied victory at **El-Alamein**, only 106km (66 miles) west of Alexandria, turned the tide.

The Birth of Modern Egypt

In 1945 Egypt was a founder member of the Arab League and in 1948 was drawn into the first **Arab-Israeli war** when the Arab states attempted to snuff out the newly formed State of Israel. The Arab defeat increased popular discontent with the incompetent and extravagant rule of King Farouk, who had come to the throne in 1936, and he was overthrown in July 1952 by an army junta dominated by **Gamal Abdel Nasser**. The Republic of Egypt was born in June 1953.

Nasser's strongly nationalist policies eventually culminated in the nationalizing of the Suez Canal. A combined British, French and Israeli invasion which was aimed at toppling Nasser and subsequently wresting control of the Canal from Egypt, failed ignominiously after an American ultimatum forced the invaders to withdraw. Nasser became a hero to the entire Arab world virtually overnight. Nasser aligned Egypt with the Union of Soviet Socialist Republics, in the process acquiring Soviet weaponry and welcoming military and technical advisers from the USSR. Soviet aid and expertise built the **Aswan High Dam**, Nasser's most enduring monument, which was completed a year after his death in 1971. Nasser's heroic status survived even the shattering defeat of the Six Day War in 1967, when Israel shattered Arab forces poised on its borders and seized Sinai from Egypt.

Gamal Abdel Nasser

Gamal Abdel Nasser (1918–70) was born in Alexandria, the son of a post office clerk. He rose to the rank of colonel in the Egyptian army and became a leader in the Free Officers' movement, which opposed both British domination and the corrupt government of Farouk. One of the leaders of the 1952 coup which overthrew Farouk, he later survived an assassination attempt to become president in 1954. In 1958 he took Egypt into the United Arab Republic, a union with Syria which collapsed three years later, though Nasser kept the title of President of the UAR. The Suez crisis of 1956 bolstered his popularity, which survived even the defeat of the 1967 war. He died in office in 1970. Even today, he is Egypt's national hero.

Nasser's successor, **Anwar Sadat**, moved Egypt away from its alliance with the USSR and sought closer links with the West. In October 1973 he launched Egyptian forces across the Suez Canal in a bid to drive the Israelis out of Sinai. Though Israel rallied and managed to push the Egyptians back, the assault helped to restore Egypt's pride that had been damaged by the defeat of 1967. It enabled Sadat to begin a peace process with Israel in 1977, culminating in the Camp David agreement and peace treaty of 1979, under which Israel withdrew from Sinai to its 1948 border with Egypt. The agreement, however, alienated Egypt's more stubborn Arab allies, who were fanatically opposed to Israel, as well as home-grown Muslim extremists, who assassinated Sadat in 1981.

Sadat's successor as president, **Hosni Mubarak**, remains in power at time of writing. Mubarak has continued Sadat's policy of *rapprochement* with the West and has liberalized the economy while permitting greater political and civil freedom. During his period in power, however, Egypt has also seen a marked increase in Islamic fundamentalism which rejects the cosmopolitan values of the west in favour of the strict dictates of the Koran. The most extreme of these Islamists carried out a campaign of terror in the mid-1990s, but in recent years the major groups have renounced violence.

MUHAMMAD ANWAR SADAT

Anwar Sadat (1921–81) played an influential part in the Free Officers' coup that brought Nasser to power, and remained a key member of Nasser's inner circle. Appointed vice president in 1969, he became president on Nasser's death. He reversed many of Nasser's less successful policies, expelling the USSR's military advisers in 1972, and in 1973 introducing economic reforms that led to price rises and riots. In 1981 he was assassinated by Islamic extremists who regarded him as a traitor to the Arab cause.

Opposite: *Allied and Axis war dead are commemorated at the cemeteries of El-Alamein.*
Left: *The High Dam at Aswan, enduring monument to strongman Gamal Abdel Nasser.*

Financial Statistics

Inflation dropped from 9.4 per cent in 1994/95 to 2.4 per cent in 2000/01. Over the same period Egypt reduced its foreign debt from US$33 billion to US$26.6 billion, and increased its foreign currency reserves from US$10.4 billion to US$14.3 billion. Unemployment has also decreased, from 9.6 per cent of the workforce in 1994/95 to 7.6 per cent in 2000/01.

GOVERNMENT AND ECONOMY

Since the ousting of Egypt's last monarch following the military coup led by Gamal Abdel Nasser in 1952, Egypt has been nominally a democratic republic. Under Nasser, however, Egypt was in effect a one-party dictatorship dominated by the **Arab Socialist Union**, and civil liberties and the media were severely curtailed. The ASU's successor, the **National Democratic Party**, remains in undisputed power, but under Nasser's successors, Anwar Sadat and **Hosni Mubarak**, there has been an easing of restrictions on the media and an easing of the NDP's tight grip on political life. Today, several small opposition parties are represented in the People's Assembly, the country's parliament, but the NDP seems unlikely to be toppled in the foreseeable future.

The head of state and the real political power is the president, elected for a six-year term (Mubarak was re-elected to a fourth term in 1999). The president is the chief of the armed forces and also appoints the vice president, prime minister, regional governors, police chiefs and other key officials, and therefore has great political patronage. Much legislation is by presidential decree, rather than by parliament, and there is no effective system of political and judicial checks and balances. The two-chamber parliament consists of an appointed **Consultative Assembly**, which has no legislative role, and the **People's Assembly**, a legislative body which is elected by universal suffrage every five years.

Below: *Dates are a staple crop in the desert oases and along the Nile.*

Government by decree has in a sense made it easier for Egypt to reverse economic policies which proved increasingly unworkable. Under Nasser, Egypt pursued the Soviet-

Above: *Shops and market stalls spill over into busy urban streets.*

style dream of a politically planned economy, with advisers from the USSR encouraging grandiose plans for modernization. There were success stories, most notably the building of the High Dam at Aswan, which assured the country of a virtually limitless supply of hydro-electric power. Overall, however, most plans failed. Nasser nationalized many industries and businesses. Among the victims of this policy was the large Greek-Egyptian community of Alexandria, most of whom chose to leave Egypt for Greece, taking their skills, capital and connections with them and virtually ending a connection between Egypt and Greece that had lasted for more than 2000 years.

Since the 1980s, the government has pursued a more liberal economic policy, easing currency controls and restrictions on private capital, encouraging inward investment and recognizing that the free market is likely to prove a more powerful modernizing force than ineffective planning from the top down.

From the late 1970s, tourism has become an important factor in the economy, not just in areas like Cairo and Luxor which have attracted well-heeled European sightseers since the 19th century, but also in areas like Hurghada and the Sinai resorts, where tourism has become the biggest source of employment and foreign revenue. The appearance of a shadowy alliance of fundamentalist Islamic terrorists, dedicated to the violent overthrow of the government and deliberately targeting the tourism industry, severely damaged Egypt's tourism for a while in the 1990s, as did the US-Iraq war of 2003, but Egypt's eternal appeal ensures a quick recovery.

EDUCATION

Schooling is compulsory from six to 12 years of age. State schools are free and there are also private and Islamic schools. Students who complete secondary education may go on to study at state universities and technical colleges, and there are also several prestigious Islamic universities in Egypt.

THE PEOPLE

More than 98 per cent of Egypt's approximately 69 million people live in the Nile Valley and in the populous, fertile Delta. And of these, at least 15 million, perhaps as many as 20 million, live in the chaotic urban sprawl of Cairo. The drift to the capital gathered pace in the 1980s and 1990s, as younger Egyptians deserted the hard agricultural labour and unchanging rhythms of village life for the brighter lights of Cairo and the country's other major cities. But Cairo's population, like that of the country as a whole, is swollen by a high birth rate and a higher life expectancy, thanks to cleaner water, better diet and improved health care. Population growth is at present around 1.33 million a year, with potentially disastrous results.

Above: *Nowadays younger Egyptians are deserting the Delta villages for the streets of Cairo and other cities.*
Below: *In the villages of Nubia, south of Aswan, village life has changed very little.*

Until Nasser's revolution, Egypt's cities – especially Alexandria and Cairo – had a **cosmopolitan** urban mix. The nationalistic fervour of the Nasserite republic, coupled with the birth of Israel, led to confiscation of 'foreign' property and the departure of the relatively large Greek and Jewish minorities. As a result, Egypt is now probably less ethnically mixed than at any time in its long history.

PEOPLE

Most Egyptians are of mixed race, descended from Arabs, ancient Egyptians, Berbers, Greeks and Turks among other races. The Nubians, in the extreme south, are a largely separate people, with their own language, and the Bedouin, who live in the deserts of Sinai and the west, are descended from Arabs from the Arabian peninsula.

There are, however, huge differences between the lives of **city-dwellers** and the villagers of the Delta and the Nile, though those differences are being steadily eroded by the technology of television and the video recorder, which bring a view (however twisted) of the outside world into even the simplest farming villages. Urban Egyptians share most of the preoccupations of city-dwellers the world over, and Cairo and Alexandria are both overwhelmingly modern cities in which the remnants of ancient and medieval Egypt sometimes seem to be in danger of being overwhelmed by the tide of traffic and new buildings. In **rural villages**, by contrast, life still proceeds at a much more traditional pace. Most people rise at dawn, and the donkey, ox-cart and sailing felucca are still more important means of transport than the pick-up truck. Any village worth the name has its mosque, and the call to prayer sets the daily rhythm. But modern road, rail and air transport means that, for village youths, the temptations of the city are never very far away.

Almost all Egyptians live in the major cities, small towns or farming villages, but a few thousand **pastoralist nomads** still roam the deserts east and west of the Nile and the barren lands of Sinai. These Bedouin herders still resist government efforts to settle them in permanent villages, and cling to a timeless way of life that has hardly changed in centuries. Almost equally timeless are the villages scattered around the fertile oases of the Western Desert, which have only recently been connected to the Nile heartland by modern roads. In the deep south, where Egypt borders Sudan, there are dark-skinned **Nubian** villagers who speak their own language and have their own distinct culture.

Another tiny ethnic minority are the people of the Siwa oasis, the descendants of **Berber** wanderers from the west who settled here centuries ago. They maintain their own language and many of their unique customs.

Sport

Soccer is Egypt's favourite sport, with Ahly and Zamalek, the two top teams (both from Cairo), arousing impassioned support. That said, Egypt has made relatively little impact on the international soccer stage. Most cities have public **swimming** pools, and **tennis** and **rowing** are popular with wealthier Egyptians. **Horse-** and **camel racing** are traditional desert sports, especially in Bedouin areas. **Scuba diving** is becoming popular with Egyptians and visitors, and **windsurfing** on the Mediterranean and Red Sea coasts has also caught on with the locals.

Below: *Bedouin desert wanderers are gradually being forced to give up their traditional way of life.*

MEDIA

All Egyptian radio and TV stations are state-owned, but satellite channels in major hotels present a less censored view of the world. There are a number of English language newspapers and magazines, including a weekly English arm of the long-established Arabic daily *Al-Ahram*, and the daily Egyptian Gazette. The press is technically free, and a number of opposition parties and groups have their own newspaper, but there is a certain amount of intimidation and self-censorship.

Opposite: *Prayers at the tomb of a Mameluke princess, Khawand Tatar el-Higaziya.*

Below: *These children are dressed for the October festival in Siwa, an oasis in the Western Desert with a distinct local language.*

Language

Arabic is the universal language of Egypt, as it is of the whole of North Africa and the Middle East. Though the Egyptian version differs considerably from, for example, Moroccan Arabic, the written form is in other respects identical across the Arabic-speaking world. Arabic script reads from right to left, and uses 29 letters. It is not always possible to transcribe Arabic letters exactly into English: the guttural sounds represented as Q, Kh, Gh, ' and ' present particular problems, and short vowels are not written. On maps and in local guides you may find place names spelt in several different ways (such as Qena/Kena, Edfu/Idfu, Saqqara/Sakkara). Use your imagination.

Egyptians may not feel themselves superior to other Arabs, but they certainly feel that they have a distinct national identity and arguably a more cosmopolitan outlook, formed by the influence of many different cultures. Until the upsurge of nationalism under Nasser, **French** was the second language of the educated professional class, and **Greek** was the first language of the long-established trading community of Alexandria, while under the British protectorate **English** was added to the linguistic portfolio. As a result, many Egyptians – and almost everyone involved in the tourist industry, from camel-men and felucca skippers to the management of luxury hotels – can speak and understand not only English but a smattering of French, German and Italian as well.

As is the case everywhere else in the world, an attempt on your part to grasp at least some of the basics will always be warmly welcomed by your Egyptian hosts (*see* Vital Phrases, page 110, and Useful Phrases, page 125).

Religion

While the constitution officially guarantees freedom of religion, **Islam** is constitutionally recognized as the official faith of Egypt. Egyptians tend to be devout without being fanatical. No village, however small, is without its mosque, and the thousand-year-old El-Azhar University in Cairo is one of the guiding lights of the (Sunni) Islamic world.

That said, Egyptian society as a whole takes a relaxed view of some of Islam's more onerous prohibitions. Even in the rural villages where Islamic tradition has a stronger hold than among the urban middle class, women are not segregated from everyday life or forced to wear the veil, though many retain the traditional headscarf.

This relaxed attitude has its opponents among fundamentalist Muslims, who wish to reimpose the letter of Koranic law on everyday life. The fundamentalist movement includes those who believe that the way to achieve this is by peaceful protest and moral example. Unfortunately, it sometimes also includes an extremist element which believes in the use of terror tactics, against tourists as well as the Egyptian political establishment, to destabilize the state. In the absence of an effective secular opposition to the ruling party, radical Islam has become a focus for younger working-class Egyptians who see the gap between rich and poor continuing to widen, despite – or perhaps because of – economic modernization.

It is during the great festivals of the Islamic calendar that Egypt is most visibly a piously Muslim culture. During **Ramadan**, the month when good Muslims fast from dawn until dusk, you may find hotel bars reluctant to serve alcohol, while restaurants and cafés outside the large hotels will be even more severely curtailed. To compensate, the festival of **Eid el-Fitr**, at the end of Ramadan, is marked by feasting, fireworks, and colourful open-air celebrations.

SUNNI AND SHIAH

Most Egyptians are Muslims of the Sunni persuasion, which triumphed over the Shiite or Fatimid version of Islam during the 8th century AD. Shiites maintain that only a descendant of the prophet Mohammed (through his daughter Fatima and son-in-law Ali) has the right to lead Islam. Both Ali and his sons Hassan and Hussein were killed in the power struggle between the Fatimids and Sunni faction (which takes a more relaxed view of secular leadership) which followed Mohammed's death. In 1153, Hussein's head was interred in the Sayyidna el-Hussein Mosque in Cairo's bazaar quarter.

Right: *Greek Orthodox monks at the door to St Catherine's Monastery.* **Opposite top:** *Ancient skills are still used by this tentmaker and mousetrap vendor in a Cairo bazaar.* **Opposite bottom:** *Garish hand-painted murals advertise the latest locally produced movies.*

COPTIC POPES

The patriarchs of the Coptic faith have struggled since its beginnings to maintain their claim to equal status with the pontiffs of the Roman Catholic, Greek Orthodox and Russian Orthodox churches, while at the same time reassuring their Muslim compatriots that Copts are Egyptian patriots too. In 1996, the Coptic Pope Shenouda III prohibited his flock from visiting the Christian places of pilgrimage in Jerusalem in protest against Israel's blocking of the Middle East peace process. It was a move clearly aimed at aligning the Copts of Egypt with the Arab camp, but as a side effect it began to turn Cairo into a 'new Jerusalem' for the Copts, with the government at long last releasing funds to restore near-derelict places of worship such as the 10th-century Hanging Church (Church of the Virgin), where a US$6.7 million restoration programme began in 1998.

About 90 per cent of the population of the country is Muslim. Most of the remaining 10 per cent cling to the **Coptic Christian** faith brought to Egypt by St Mark almost 2000 years ago. The Coptic liturgy and ceremonial are very similar to those of the Greek and Russian Orthodox churches, and like Orthodox Christianity, the Coptic Church is strongly monastic. The adherence of the Egyptian Church to the Monophysite doctrine, which held that there was only one nature in Christ, led to its eventual split from mainstream Christianity in AD451. Coptic isolation was made permanent by the conquest of Egypt by Islam. Today, the monasteries of the Western Desert are the heart of the Coptic tradition, but several historic churches survive in Cairo and in Alexandria.

Art and Culture

Little is known for sure of ancient Egyptian art. What can be seen is that the painters whose work illuminates the walls of millennia-old tombs had a marvellous grasp of flowing line and brilliant colour, while their skill in blending pigments means that their paintings today are almost as vivid as the day they were painted (*see* also page 17).

Modern arts in Egypt have suffered from a lack of both government subsidy and of private sponsorship, and outside of Cairo there is little of cultural note that is

Music

Egypt dances to many rhythms, though it is sometimes hard for the tourist to get away from the ersatz belly-dance shows put on in many hotels. ***Saidi***, the music of the Nile Valley, is rhythmic, featuring a drum called the *naharsan* and a clarinet-like wooden trumpet, the *mismar saidi*. Each region of the country has its own music: ***fellahi*** from the Delta villages, ***sawahlee*** from the Mediterranean coast, **Nubian**, **Bedouin** and **classical**, though admittedly the uneducated Western ear may have trouble telling them apart. ***Jeel***, which combines western pop influences with traditional rhythms, is hugely popular with the urban young.

readily accessible to the visitor. Even in the capital, suitable venues for either highbrow or popular cultural events are conspicuous by their absence. The once-thriving Egyptian cinema industry, which made movies not just for Egypt but for the entire Arabic-speaking world, has been quite hard hit by the advent of video and satellite TV in all its key markets. The traditional Islamic prohibition on the representation of living creatures historically hampered development of the visual arts, and more recently, fundamentalist Islam has proven a powerfully repressive force, frowning on virtually every form of modern art, cinema, theatre, and literature.

In 1996, Egypt scored an international artistic triumph with the dramatic staging of Verdi's opera *Aïda* in the Temple of Karnak at Luxor – a most appropriate venue – and the same opera is now produced every one or two years in front of the Pyramids at Giza. In Cairo, events outside the entertainment which is provided at standard tourist hotels include imported opera and orchestral performances at the new **Cairo Opera House** and theatre performances in English as well as Arabic at the **Gumhuria Theatre** and at the new **Falaki Theatre** in the American University. Belly dancing is staged especially for the entertainment of tourists in the nightclubs attached to the main hotels.

Soft Drinks

Because Egypt is a Muslim country where many people do not touch alcohol, and where many more cannot afford expensive canned soft drinks, there are dozens of local juice drinks for sale at stands on every street. What is on sale depends on what is in season, but as well as familiar favourites such as orange, guava, banana or lime you can sample sugar cane, tamarind or more exotic beverages made from licorice, hibiscus, carob bean, fenugreek or aniseed.

Food and Drink

Traditional Egyptian cooking takes many forms. Everyday street snacks include **taamiya** (also called felafel and found throughout the Middle East), tasty deep-fried nuggets of mashed beans flavoured with herbs and spices. Another speciality of everyday street fare in Egypt is **kushari**, a bowl of noodles, rice and lentils topped with a spicy tomato sauce. The staple, national dish is **fuul**, a rich and flavoursome blend of stewed fava beans with sesame oil, lemon, salt and pepper, and served with salad and bread. Other dips and vegetable mixes include **tahina**, made from pulped sesame seeds, and **baba ghanoug**, made from eggplant and tahina.

For ordinary Egyptians, whether in the cities or in the villages, meat is not something to be eaten every day but a treat for special occasions. Lamb, mutton, chicken and pigeon are the most prominent items on the festive menu. **Kofta**, **kebab** and **shawarma** are available in most Egyptian restaurants and are commonly made with lamb. In Alexandria and also on the Red Sea coast, fish is plentiful and varied, and is usually served grilled, but **bolti** (Nile perch) also appears on the menu in Cairo and the Nile Valley towns. **Desserts** are usually sticky and sweet, often made with many layers of pastry and honey.

Tourist hotels offer international-style cuisine, usually in buffet form. Although no Egyptian would readily consume pork products, sausage, bacon and salami can

Below: *This man is making taamiya – the cheap, tasty and nutritious staple snack of Egyptian streets.*

be found on the breakfast buffet of every major tourist hotel.

Egypt's relaxed approach to Islam means alcohol is much more freely available than in most Islamic countries, and indeed the country produces its own wines, beers and spirits. A number of local beers are now available, including Egypt's famed Stella lager and the darker, tastier Stella Premium and the popular Sakkara Gold. Egyptian wine has benefited remarkably from recent privatization and new products, and there are some quite palatable wines on the market: the grand old names of Omar Khayyam (red), Rubis d'Egypte (rosé), and Cru des Ptolemées (white) still dominate, all from the famous Gianaclis vineyard, but the Obelisk red and white are also popular, and the Grand Marquis red and white have added a touch of class. There is now even a perfectly resepctable Egyptian sparkling wine, Aida. Egypt also produces Greek-style, aniseed-flavoured **ouzo**, a strong white spirit which turns milky when water is added, and also an Egyptian variant on ouzo called **zebib**. Both are definitely acquired tastes. Imported beers, wines and spirits are on offer at all the larger tourist hotels and restaurants, but these drinks cost considerably more than the local versions.

Egyptian-style **coffee** is similar to that found in Greece and Turkey, and is served strong, sweet, and in tiny cups. It is sometimes also flavoured with cardamom seeds. **Tea** usually comes black and in small glasses, and most Egyptians like it very, very sweet, sometimes adding five or six spoonfuls of sugar.

Above: *For the desert Bedouin, making tea for a guest is an elaborate ceremony.*

'Drinking' Tobacco

Most Egyptian men, and some women, are inveterate smokers. Egyptians talk of 'drinking' tobacco and there are still plenty of corner cafés where patrons can sample a fill of plain or flavoured tobacco in a 'shisha', the tall, glass and brassware water pipe favoured by traditionalists. Though cooled by the water it bubbles through, the strong tobacco produces a distinct buzz.

2
Cairo

Egypt's capital, with its startling blend of old and new, has to be taken on its own terms. Cairo's teeming crowds, horrendous traffic and air pollution and general lack of organization can be intimidating. That said, so many of the country's most fantastic sights are here that a visit to Cairo is truly the key to understanding Egypt.

Cairo is a city of at least 15 million, perhaps 20 million people (accurate figures are hard to come by). The largest city in Africa, and one of the largest in the world, the Egyptian capital is home to around a quarter of the country's total population. Bisected by the Nile, its urban sprawl has expanded in all directions to lap at the very feet of the pyramids, while the churches, mosques and fortifications of the original city, dating from the time of Saladin and the Fatimid Caliphs, are surrounded by a modern maze of offices, factories, motorways and tenement blocks. Cairo typifies Egypt, stretching as it does from the banks of the Nile into the desert on either side.

The modern city centre, with most of the large tourist hotels and commercial and government buildings, is on the east bank, and its heart is **Midan el-Tahrir** (Liberation Square). Medieval Cairo, embracing the **Citadel**, **El-Azhar** and other mosques, and the **Khan el-Khalili Bazaar** area, is east of the modern city centre, 3km (2 miles) from the river. The heart of **Coptic Cairo** is the **Misr el-Qadima** area, on the east bank south of the centre. **Giza** is about 10km (6 miles) southwest of the city centre. **Saqqara** is 20km (12 miles) south of Giza and the ruins of **Memphis** are 6km (3.5 miles) east of Saqqara.

DON'T MISS

*** **Pyramids of Giza:** the most potent symbols of ancient Egypt.
*** **Sphinx:** newly restored to its ancient grandeur.
*** **Egyptian Antiquities Museum:** fantastic collection of rare treasures.
** **Pyramids of Saqqara:** incredible aura of antiquity and mystery.
** **Citadel of Saladin:** mighty fortress walls and historic mosque.

Opposite: *The Mohammed Ali Mosque, begun in 1830 and completed in 1848.*

Cairo Climate

Cairo has a desert climate and in summer its heat and dust are aggravated by man-made pollution. Avoid **high summer** (June–August). Winter days are warm but nights can be very chilly. Best times to visit are spring and autumn. **Rain** is very rare at any time of year.

Central Cairo

Modern Cairo is bisected by the Nile, which runs south-north through the city. Two long, thin islands, **Roda** and **Gezira**, are connected to both banks of the river by bridges, and on these stand several of Cairo's less visited museums. There are relatively few sights to see in this modern part of town, but the **Egyptian Antiquities Museum** is essential viewing.

Egyptian Antiquities Museum ★★★

The museum is situated to the north of Midan el-Tahrir. Do not miss this fantastic collection. Starting with relics of the Old Kingdom on the ground floor, a clockwise tour takes you through a range of finds from the Middle and New Kingdom dynasties and finally the Hellenistic-Roman era. The first floor houses most of the treasures from the tomb of **Tutankhamun**, and the mummies of **Ramses II** and other Pharaohs can be seen in the Mummy Room. There are various guide books available to help you navigate your way around. Open 09:00–18:45; closed Friday 11:15–13:30.

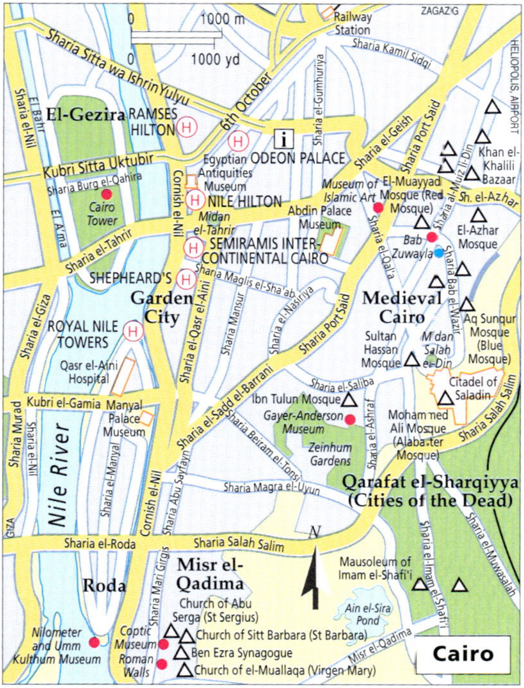

Cairo Tower ★

Situated at Sharia Burg el-Qahira, Gezira Island. A prominent 187m (613.5ft) landmark, the tower has an observation platform with excellent views of the vast sprawl of Cairo. On a clear day (more likely in winter than in smoggy summer) you may be able to see as far as the Great Pyramids. The night-time panorama from the enclosed café-restaurant at the top of the tower is even more spectacular. Open 09:00–00:00.

Above: *The Cairo Tower overlooks the city centre and the Nile.*

Manyal Palace Museum *

Located at Sharia Ahmed Abdel Rahim, Roda Island. Built for King Farouk's uncle in 1903, this rococo palace, lavishly decorated within and cluttered with ornate furniture, gilt mirrors, heavy drapes, rather gaudy glassware, brass and silverware in profusion, is indicative of the royal extravagance amid poverty that ultimately led to the overthrow of the Dynasty and the establishment of the Republic. Open 09:00–16:00.

Nilometer **

Situated on the southern tip of Roda Island. There would have been a Nilometer here in Pharaonic times, although the present structure was built only in the 9th century. The high-water marks on the central octagonal stone column of the Nilometer were used to gauge the extent of each season's floods, and therefore to predict the harvests. Taxes could then be set accordingly.

In contrast to the teeming squalor of central Cairo are the more affluent suburbs of the city's northern and western fringe. **Heliopolis**, to the north of the centre, is the site of one of the oldest settlements in Egypt, of which nothing now remains. The modern suburb was originally built to house wealthy European expatriates and has become the home of a native Egyptian moneyed class, where luxury apartment blocks stand next to villas hidden behind high walls. Over the last 20 to 30 years **Giza**, southwest of the city centre, has grown to become a fully fledged suburb and houses a less affluent middle class in a sprawl of nondescript high-rise buildings.

King Farouk

The name of the last king of modern Egypt is still a byword for excess almost half a century after his downfall. Caught between British power and nationalist populism, Farouk took little responsibility for his kingdom, preferring fast cars, casinos, horse racing, luxury yachts and glamorous women, while his corrupt ministers lined their pockets at the expense of the country. King Farouk's fondness for the opposite sex was legendary. Reputedly, his favourite aphrodisiac and morning-after pick-me-up was made by simmering the stock from 300 pigeons to reduce it to a half-litre of strong consommé. He died in exile in Switzerland in 1965.

Baksheesh

Self-appointed 'guides' will point out the obvious in English as fragmentary as the ruins. Perhaps the biggest fly in the ointment of Egyptian tourism is 'baksheesh'. It is not quite like tipping, which implies some service; it literally means 'share the wealth' and signifies that tourists should do just that, regardless of whether a service has been performed, or even requested. Doormen, ticket collectors, taxi drivers, boatmen, camel drivers, porters, and guides will expect baksheesh. And why not? By the standard of most Egyptians, even budget travellers are wealthy. Most don't expect much. Just make sure you have plenty of small change.

Medieval Cairo

Citadel of Saladin **

Begun by Saladin in 1176, this complex of massive fortifications, situated on a hill above the Midan Salah el-Din, is one of the city's main landmarks, and was the home of Egypt's rulers until the mid-19th century. The walls of the Citadel enclose three historic mosques and several small museums. Citadel and museums open 09:00–16:00, closed Friday 11:15–13:15.

Mohammed Ali Mosque (Alabaster Mosque) **

Egypt's first modernizing ruler began this grand Ottoman-style mosque with its enormous central dome, delicate minarets and supporting half-domes, in 1830. Crowning the low hill the Citadel stands on, it was completed in 1848, just before Mohammed Ali's death, and his tomb is within. The interior is remarkably light and decorated with geometric patterns and Koranic inscriptions.

Also in the southern enclosure of the Citadel is the **Palace of Mohammed Ali (El-Gawhara Palace)**, built in 1814. Supercilious Pashas stare from 19th-century princely portraits in this former royal palace, on display with a collection of overstuffed furniture and dusty costumes. The Harim Palace in the northern enclosure was

Below: *The Mosque of Mohammed Ali dominates the medieval Citadel.*

once the private residence of Mohammed Ali, and now houses the **Military Museum**, containing a collection of medals, banners, musical instruments, photographs, uniforms and documents. The grand carriages used by the Khedives are on display nearby in the **Carriage Museum**. The **National Police Museum**, also in the northern enclosure, contains a rogues' gallery of Egypt's most famous criminals. There is a good view of Islamic Cairo and some of the city's most historic mosques from the parapets of the Citadel behind the National Police Museum.

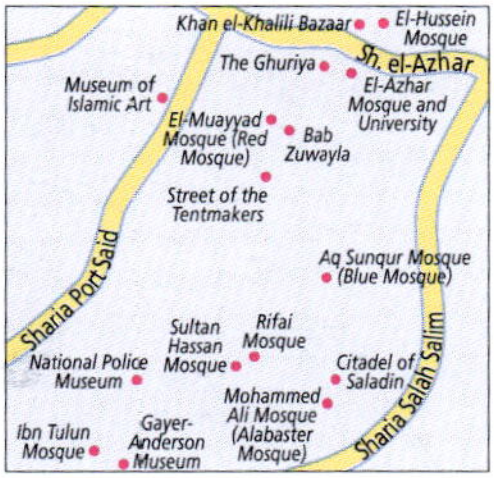

Ibn Tulun Mosque **

Situated on Sharia el-Saliba to the west of the Citadel. Perhaps the city's most spectacular mosque, and one of the largest in the world, it has a unique minaret with an exterior spiral staircase, and an enormous central courtyard where thousands gather to pray. It was built by the 9th-century Wali (governor) Ibn Tulun. Open 09:00–16:00. Adjacent to the outer court of the Ibn Tulun Mosque is the Gayer-Anderson Museum. These two medieval houses, knocked into one by an early 20th-century English resident, now form part of the Museum of Islamic Art. The annexe is interesting particularly for its traditional architecture as well as its clutter of Oriental furniture and antiques. Open 09:00–16:00, closed Fridays 11:15–13:15.

Sultan Hassan Mosque **

Situated below the Citadel on the Midan Salah el-Din. Masonry from the Great Pyramids of Giza was believed to have been used to build this 14th-century mosque decreed by a Mameluke Sultan. The interior is bare so that worshippers should not be distracted from their prayers. Open 09:00–16:00.

Aq Sunqur Mosque (Blue Mosque) *

Sharia Bab el-Wazir. Built in the 14th century, the ceramic tiles used to decorate the walls from which the mosque gets its name were added in the 1650s. A stretch of the medieval city wall has been preserved and runs northeast from the mosque. Open 09:00–16:00.

THE SCRIBE OF CAIRO

The development of an authentic Egyptian literature has been handicapped by a low literacy rate (fewer than one in two Egyptians can read) and by censorship under both British rule and the one-party state of Nasser and Sadat. Even under Mubarak's more liberal regime, there is a high degree of self censorship, with tacit limits on criticism of the government and of resurgent Islam. The reputation of the father of modern Egyptian literature, **Naguib Mahfouz** (b.1911), rests as much on lack of contemporary competitors as on literary skill. Mahfouz's best known work, *The Cairo Trilogy*, follows the life of a prosperous Cairo merchant family from the end of World War I to the end of World War II; his later works, however, were less well received. He was dubbed 'The Scribe of Cairo', and the *Trilogy* brought his works to a wider, international audience. He received the **Nobel Prize for Literature** in 1988.

Bab Zuwayla and El-Muayyad Mosque **

On the Sharia el-Muizz. Bab Zuwayla, once the southern towered gate of medieval Cairo, is one of only three gates which remain of the 60 that once pierced the city walls. Together with most of the walls, the rest of the gates were demolished during the 19th century to allow the city to expand. The gate has its own mosque. The twin minarets of the 15th-century **Mosque of el-Muayyad**, also known as the **Red Mosque**, form part of the gate, with a doorway of black and white marble and massive wood and bronze doors opening into the mosque. Open 09:00–16:00.

Museum of Islamic Art **

Located on the corner of Sharia Port Said and Sharia el-Qal'a. This is not so much a museum of 'fine art' in the Western sense as of craftsmanship and decoration, with furniture and woodwork, carvings, illuminated books, ceramics and copper and brassware from every era and corner of the Muslim world. Open 09:00–16:00, closed Friday 11:15–13:15.

El-Azhar

More than 1000 years old, El-Azhar University still wields colossal influence across the entire Islamic world. Its students, who number more than 20,000, are not only from Egypt and neighbouring Arab countries but from Muslim nations as far away as Indonesia and Malaysia in the east and Mauretania and Morocco in the west. The university also attracts Islamic scholars from Muslim communities in Europe, East and Southern Africa and North America. Foreign students receive free lodging and many benefit from scholarships endowed over the centuries by wealthy philanthropists.

El-Azhar Mosque and University ***

Sharia el-Azhar, 3km (2 miles) east of Midan el-Tahrir. Completed in AD971, El-Azhar is both mosque and theological university, and the leading centre of learning of orthodox Sunni Islam. Successive rulers vied to endow El-Azhar with new buildings and faculties, and as well as its venerable schools of Koranic study it has more recently expanded to include departments of medicine and science. The Koran, however, is still studied, as it has been for more than a thousand years, beneath the pillars of the central court, where scholars of Islam sit cross-legged around their teachers. Open 09:00–15:00, closed Friday 11:00–13:00.

Khan el-Khalili Bazaar ***

Enter via the corner of Sharia el-Muski and Sharia el-Muizz. Khan el-Khalili is far more than a tourist attraction. In many ways it is still the true heart of Cairo, throbbing to a steady beat from dawn until midnight and after. The bazaar first opened for business in 1382 and hardly seems to have closed since. It is not just a shopping area, but the home of many thousands of Cairenes, and when your feet get tired you can join them for a pipe of apple-flavoured tobacco or a glass of cardamom-scented coffee in one of dozens of cafés tucked away in lanes and alleys redolent with perfumes, spices, charcoal smoke and new leather goods.

Water pipes and brassware, rugs and carpets, antique furniture and musical instruments are sold in the narrow lanes of the bazaar area alongside herbs, spices, foodstuffs and more mundane household goods. There are many pavement cafés and tea shops. Allow plenty of time to explore, get lost and haggle over souvenirs.

Don't Buy

Many Egyptian animal species are protected, but that doesn't seem to stop specimens ending up stuffed in the souks. Examples of products you should not buy include anything made from **gazelle hide**, **crocodile** or **snakeskin**, or **turtle shell**. You may also see **ivory** smuggled from Sudan, Uganda or Kenya. International trade in all these products is banned under the CITES agreement, to which the EU nations, the US, and most other countries are signatories. Attempts to bring such products home will mean confiscation by Customs and/or a heavy fine.

Qarafat el-Sharqiyya (Eastern Cemetery, also known as the Cities of the Dead) **

About 1km (0.5 mile) east of El-Azhar mosque. Collectively known as the **Cities of the Dead**, the cemeteries occupying the space north and south of the Citadel offer a striking contrast between the lavishly decorated resting places of medieval Caliphs and the lifestyle of the poorest of Cairo's poor, thousands of whom make their homes in and among the stone tombs. The most important cemetery is the Eastern Cemetery (north of the Citadel). The domed mausoleum of the Mameluke ruler Qaytbay was built in 1474, and encloses a high and ornately carved and painted tomb chamber. The dome is adorned outside with abstract geometric patterns. Open 08:00–16:00.

Opposite: *Bab Zuwayla is one of the three remaining city gates of Cairo.*
Below: *Almost anything can be bought from the bazaar stalls, but haggling is* de rigueur.

Above: *Copts (Egyptian Christians) always celebrate Christmas with age-old ceremony.*

Coptic Cairo

A great number of Cairo's surviving Coptic churches, as well as relics of the Roman city, can be found in the Misr el-Qadima quarter, centre of Coptic Christianity in Cairo.

Church of Abu Serga (St Sergius) ⋆

Off Sharia Mari Girgis, Misr el-Qadima. A plaque on the church wall claims that the Holy Family sheltered here (or in the cave which forms the crypt) after the flight into Egypt. Abu Serga is one of Egypt's oldest Coptic places of worship, dating from the 5th century. Open 08:00–16:00.

Church of Sitt Barbara (St Barbara) ⋆

Off Sharia Mari Girgis, Misr el-Qadima. This 11th-century church contains the relics of the martyred St Barbara, who was executed by the Romans in the 3rd century AD. Open 08:00–16:00.

Ben Ezra Synagogue ⋆

The synagogue is situated next to the Church of St Barbara. The oldest of the handful of synagogues that survive in Egypt, this may originally have been a church. It is entered via a gateway carved with the six-pointed Star of David. Open 08:00–16:00.

Church of el-Muallaqa (Virgin Mary) ⋆⋆

Situated near the Mari Girgis metro station, Misr el-Qadima. This is possibly the oldest Christian church in Egypt, and the most beautiful, with fine, elaborately carved stonework and, within, elegant panels of cedar and lovely ivory work altar screens. Icons of the Virgin

Perfumes

Perfumes and essences have been part of Egyptian culture since Pharaonic times, when **aromatic resins** such as frankincense and myrrh were important trade items and were used in mummifying the bodies of kings and nobles. Whole streets in the bazaar areas of Cairo and Alexandria are devoted to selling perfumes, either as raw essences, blocks of solid resin, or oils. Powerful scents such as attar of roses or patchouli oil are preferred to more subtle fragrances.

and saints adorn the walls. Also known as the 'Hanging Church', el-Muallaqa stands on beams supported by the twin gate-towers of the Roman wall. Open 08:00–16:00.

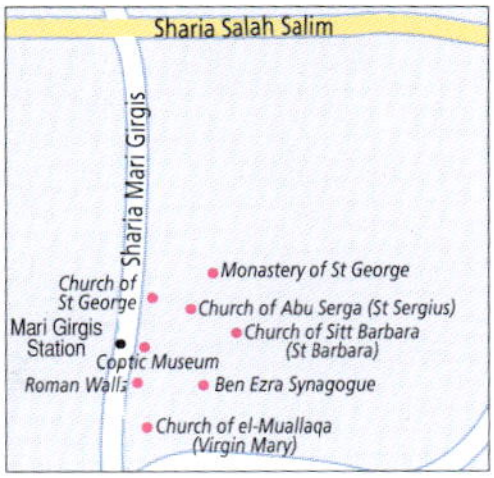

Coptic Museum **

Opposite Mari Girgis metro station, Sharia Mari Girgis. This interesting museum contains relics of the Christian heyday in Egypt during the later Roman Empire and into medieval times, with icons and religious paintings and tapestries, manuscripts and carvings. One of the most fascinating aspects of the Coptic Museum is the evidence in carvings and icons of artistic continuity with pre-Christian Egypt; even the Egyptian ankh, the symbol of immortality, may have influenced the Christian symbol of the cross. Coptic art reached its high point between the 5th and 7th centuries, from the split with the rest of the Church until the dawn of Islam. Open 09:00–16:00, closed Friday 11:00–13:00.

Roman Walls *

Opposite Mari Girgis metro station, Sharia Mari Girgis; part of Coptic Museum. The twin towers were once the Nile gateway to the walled Roman stronghold which was demolished in the 19th century. The gate opened directly onto the river, which has since changed its course. The fortress was built by Octavian to secure his hold on Egypt after defeating Cleopatra and Mark Anthony. Open 09:00–16:00, closed Friday 11:00–13:00.

Below: *Icons of Coptic saints for sale at one of Cairo's churches.*

VERDI IN CAIRO

Verdi's opera *Aïda* premiered in Cairo on 24 December 1871, after the Khedive of Egypt, Ismail Pasha, invited the Italian composer to write an opera for the inauguration of the 1000-seat **Theatre de l'Opera** which he had commissioned two years before. Verdi in turn was inspired by the eminent French Egyptologist **Auguste Mariette**, who was later appointed to design the sets and costumes for the opera's first performance. In recent years, *Aïda* has been performed both at the Pyramids and at the Temple of Karnak in Luxor.

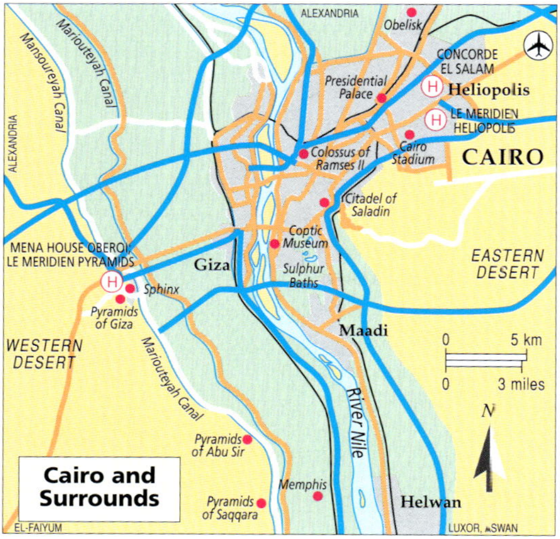

Giza

Giza is situated 11km (7 miles) southwest of Central Cairo. The suburb of Giza spreads out across what was, until recently, agricultural land, to an arid plateau on which stand the most famous and enigmatic of all the relics of ancient Egypt: the **Great Pyramids**, a challenge to Egyptologists and the inspiration of a hundred theories. There are three main pyramids at Giza, each with its outcrop of satellite pyramids where the queens of the Pharaohs were interred. Pyramid building began with the 3rd Dynasty, when the Pharaoh Zoser commissioned the architect Imhotep to build him a lasting monument of stone at Saqqara, south of Giza. More than 80 pyramids were built at **Saqqara** and other sites along the Nile, but it is the larger and better preserved Pyramids of Giza that have caught and kept the public imagination. Dawn over the Pyramids is one of the all-time great holiday experiences, and the **Sound and Light Show** with performances every evening is well worth experiencing. Each of the Great Pyramids is aligned precisely 8.5 degrees west of magnetic north, and their builders probably positioned them by the Pole Star. The significance of their location and their proportions continues to give rise to speculation. Pyramids, temples and Sphinx open 08:30–16:30.

Opposite: *Rising from the Giza plateau (left to right) are the pyramids of Cheops, Chephren and Mycerinus.*

Camels

At Giza and Luxor, in Sinai, and elsewhere, you will meet camel drivers keen to persuade you to take a trip on the ship of the desert. The one-humped dromedary may be a relatively recent arrival (camels are conspicuously absent from ancient paintings and inscriptions) but it is still inevitably associated with Egypt, and especially with the Bedouin nomads of Sinai and the Eastern Desert. Several specialist tour operators also offer longer desert safaris by camel. Be warned: the camel is one of the least comfortable mounts known to man.

Great Pyramid of Cheops ***

This is the largest of the three main Pyramids of Giza. When built, the Pyramids were encased in polished limestone and granite. This was a convenient source of ready-dressed stone for later builders. As a result, the

Pyramid of Cheops has been stripped of its fine covering, exposing course after course of dressed limestone blocks – 2.5 million of them – rising to a peak 137m (450ft) above the sands. Within, the **Great Gallery** rises to the **King's Chamber**, a clammy, empty cavern. Bereft of inscriptions or paintings, its sarcophagus is empty – be prepared for this after the awe-inspiring exterior. Just east of the Pyramid of Cheops stand three small pyramids collectively known as the **Pyramids of the Queens** and containing the tombs of Cheops' wives and sisters, as well as a cluster of empty, house-like mastabas (tombs) dating from the 4th and 5th Dynasties. Many more of these mastabas stand to the west of the pyramid, forming a stark city of the dead.

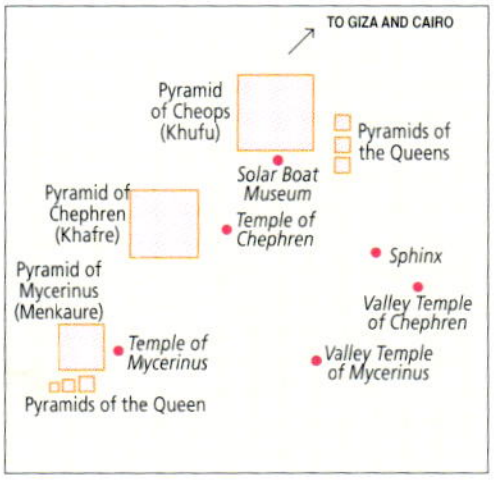

Solar Boat Museum **

Immediately south of the Great Pyramid of Cheops is the Solar Boat Museum, built out of glass to house one of two funeral barques unearthed in good condition from one of the boat pits around the Pyramid in 1954. Debate continues as to the use and significance of such vessels, which were apparently commonly buried in sealed pits within pyramid walls. They may have been used for priestly pilgrimages, or to assist the deceased Pharaoh in his voyage to the afterworld. Visitors are asked to wear special footwear to avoid tracking sand into the museum.

AIDA AT GIZA

One of the high points of the Egyptian cultural year is the performance of Verdi's opera *Aïda* amid the grandiose surroundings of one of the ancient temple sites. The opera attracts crowds of more than 90,000 visitors from all over the world despite the high prices of the tickets. The event is usually staged in October.

Above: *The Sphinx re-emerged in 1998 from a painstaking restoration programme.*

The Sphinx ★★★

This colossal figure is thought to have been commissioned by **Chephren**, son of Cheops. Sculpted from a solid block of stone, it has the body of a lion and the head of a god, or a godlike man (possibly Chephren). It stands an awesome 20m (66ft) high. The limestone rock is heavily eroded, and the Sphinx has suffered many indignities – its features were shot or chiselled off in the 14th century, and its beard, shot away by Turkish gunners, is in the British Museum. Nevertheless it is a striking sight, and is the focus of the nightly Sound and Light Show, playing the role of the narrator.

Temple of Chephren ★★

Built of red granite from Aswan, the squared columns of Chephren's valley temple, next to the Sphinx, were buried by sand and escaped most of the ravages of time. It is the best preserved of the Giza temples.

Restoring the Sphinx

In 1998 restoration experts completed a ten-year project to repair the Sphinx, which had been badly damaged by thousands of years of erosion, vandalism and more recently air pollution – but also by misguided earlier efforts at restoration. (Blocks from the statue's left shoulder fell away in 1988. The earliest restoration of the Sphinx was during the time of the Ptolemies, more than 2000 years ago.) The purpose of the man-headed, lion-bodied statue still puzzles archaeologists, but the human head is thought to symbolize intelligence while the leonine body stands for power and kingship.

Pyramid of Chephren ★★★

Almost as large as that of Cheops at 136m (446ft), this pyramid actually looks larger, because it has kept much of its polished limestone cladding and because its foundation is on higher ground. Like the Pyramid of Cheops, it is empty. A ruined funerary temple stands next to the pyramid.

Pyramid of Mycerinus ★★

This smaller pyramid, 66m (217ft) high, stands southwest of its larger relatives and is cased partly in red granite imported from Aswan. The gash in its northern flank was made by Mamelukes seeking its presumed wealth. British archaeologists finally found a way in to the funeral chamber in 1817, but the stone sarcophagus they found sank with the ship carrying it back to Britain – an inspiration for tales of curses left by dead Pharaohs to protect their tombs.

SAQQARA

Though Giza feels almost suburban, the tide of Cairo has not reached as far as Saqqara, 19km (11.5 miles) south of Giza and 30km (19 miles) from Cairo, and as a result this cluster of tombs and pyramids seems a little more remote. It is also marginally less peopled by touts, guides, souvenir sellers and men offering camel rides than its more popular neighbour. It is certainly less crowded. All sites open 09:00–17:00.

Above: *The Step Pyramid of Zoser was built more than 4500 years ago.*

Pyramid of Zoser ***

The ziggurat-like Pyramid of Zoser, or **Step Pyramid**, was built for the 3rd Dynasty Pharaoh and dates from around 2700BC, predating the Giza complex by some 200 years. This is the earliest form of pyramid, and is in fact a tiered stack of square **mastabas** (chambered tombs). Imhotep's design inspired later pyramid builders, who went on to achieve a more regular form with improved engineering. Zoser's pyramid stands in the centre of a large necropolis and is surrounded by a complex of walls and courtyards decorated with friezes showing the Pharaoh and his many achievements. Not the least of these achievements is the pyramid itself, which is one of the earliest known stone-built structures (the mastabas that surround it are built of mud brick).

Pyramid of Unas **

The exterior of this slightly smaller pyramid (a few hundred metres southwest of Zoser's pyramid) is in poor condition. Inside, however, it is more interesting. The walls of the inner chamber, unlike most of the larger pyramids, are a mass of **hieroglyphs** inspired by the Osiris cult which enjoyed popularity during the reign of Unas, the last ruler of the 5th Dynasty.

FLINDERS PETRIE

William Matthew Flinders Petrie (1853–1942) was the doyen of Egyptologists, starting his work in 1881 with a survey of the Pyramids and revealing most of what we now know of prehistoric Egypt. Petrie was painstakingly methodical (unlike most of those who preceded him) and he virtually created archaeology as a modern science, either founding or reforming every aspect of the discipline and shattering the belief that the past could only be properly known through documentary evidence. He was knighted for his work in 1923.

Tomb Robbers

Robbers and vandals continue to steal and damage Egypt's antiquities even today, encouraged by a growing market for smuggled ancient artworks. In the fight to protect the country's heritage, the National Security Department is registering temple and tomb sites using state-of-the-art video and digital photography. Some 40,000 have now been registered with the Antiquities Registration Centre, but Egypt's sheer wealth of antiquities means the task is huge.

Serapeum ★

About 1km (0.5 mile) northwest of the Pyramid of Zoser, this labyrinth was built underground to entomb the sacred bulls of Apis, believed to be incarnations of the god **Ptah**. They are more recent than the nearby pyramids: the earliest date from the time of Ramses II, but those that can be seen are from the Hellenistic era of the Ptolemies. The cult of Ptah may have a connection with the bull-worshipping civilization of Minoan Crete, which collapsed around 1750BC. Temporarily closed.

Mastaba of Mereruka ★★

Two smaller pyramids, those of **Userkaf** and **Teti**, stand just northeast of Zoser's pyramid. Immediately north of these, the multi-chambered tomb of Mereruka, a 6th-Dynasty vizier, is adorned with scenes of everyday life and opens a fascinating window on the interests and pastimes of the ancient world. **Mereruka** himself is shown painting, hunting, and playing a chess-like board game. Next to the statue of Mereruka, which stands in the final chamber, are scenes depicting the taming of wild animals, including goats, gazelles and leopards.

Opposite: *This colossal statue can be seen at the Memphis Museum.*
Below: *Hieroglyphs inside the tomb complex of the High Priest of Teti – Mastaba of Kagemni.*

Mastaba of Ti ★★

Beside the Serapeum, this tomb is interesting for the insight it offers into life in the 5th Dynasty, when Ti was a high-ranking court official. Ti, along with his wife and son, was buried here, and the tomb inscriptions show them preparing food and hunting hippopotami as well as sacrificing to the gods.

Mastaba of Akhti-Hotep and Ptah-Hotep ★★

Around 100m (109yd) west of the Pyramid of Zoser, vividly colourful tomb carvings are the most attractive asset of this dual tomb which was built for the vizier Akhti-Hotep and his son, the high priest Ptah-Hotep. The unfinished reliefs in the entrance corridor show the various stages of completion. Within, the tomb chamber has reliefs of Ptah-Hotep in priestly dress, while on the left wall are some lively scenes including children at play and cattle grazing, and also Ptah-Hotep among his servants and pet animals.

MEMPHIS

About 32km (20 miles) south of Cairo, 6km (3.5 miles) east of Saqqara. Strategically placed where the Nile Valley meets the Nile Delta, Memphis was the capital of the Old Kingdom. Even after the New Kingdom dynasties relocated the hub of their empire to **Luxor (Thebes)**, Memphis remained the greatest city of Lower Egypt until the time of the **Hellenic Ptolemies**, who founded and ruled from **Alexandria**. Memphis is said to have been founded by Menes and as such was the first Imperial city on earth.

Most of Memphis has now returned to the Nile mud from which it was built. There is so little left of the ancient city that it is hardly worth a visit in its own right, but is usually included in sightseeing tours to nearby Saqqara. Open 09:00–17:00.

Colossus of Ramses II ★

Two colossal statues of this great Pharaoh of the Old Kingdom were excavated at this site in 1820. One of them now stands in front of Cairo's central railway station. The second lies prone inside a hangar-like building which is surrounded by attractive gardens where other, much smaller statues are displayed. The most striking of these is a marble sphinx dating from the New Kingdom.

Mummification beds ★

These stone trenches opposite the Colossus gardens were used to prepare the bulls of Apis for mummification and burial in the Serapeum at Saqqara.

PTAH AND APIS

One of the oldest gods, **Ptah** gave Egypt its name (Memphis was Hukaptah – 'house of the soul of Ptah' – which went into Greek as Aigyptos). He was the patron god of Memphis and craftsmen, and appears as a man with a shaven head and a sceptre of power. **Apis**, his herald, is pictured as a bull bearing the disc of the sun. The sacred bulls, Apis's representatives on earth, were mummified and buried within the **Serapeum** at Saqqara.

Cairo at a Glance

Best Times To Visit

Cairo is pleasantest in **winter** and **spring** (November to April), with warm days and cool, even chilly nights. The hot weather begins in May, and from June to September the city is unpleasantly hot day and night, with the heat made more oppressive by severe air pollution. **Rain** is rare at any time of year. However, in a city of 15 million people, even large numbers of tourists are a drop in the bucket, and visitors to Cairo must be prepared for severe traffic congestion and bustling streets at any time of year.

Getting There

International **flights** from most European capitals and connections to cities throughout Africa and the Middle East, with rather fewer flights to the USA and Australia. Internal flights by state-owned **EgyptAir** connect Cairo with Alexandria, Luxor, Aswan, Abu Simbel, Hurghada, and Sharm el-Sheikh. There is a growing network of flights by private airlines in competition with EgyptAir on the most popular internal routes, including **Hurghada**, **Luxor**, **Aswan**, and **Sharm el-Sheikh**. Long-distance **bus services** connect Cairo with towns and cities throughout Egypt. Modern **highways** run north to Alexandria (skirting the Delta, the desert highway is a spectacular drive), south along the Nile as far as Aswan, and east to Suez and Sinai. Road travel can be hair-raising as vehicles are ill-maintained and drivers have scant regard for the rules of road safety. If you are planning to rent a **car**, always be extremely alert at the wheel. At the time of writing, visitors to Upper Egypt were encouraged to travel in **convoys** guarded by armed police because of the risk of terrorist attacks.

Rail services connect Cairo's main Ramses Station with Alexandria and run south along the Nile as far as Aswan. Rail travel is slow and not all trains are air-conditioned. **First-class express trains** take two hours from Cairo to Alexandria, 9 hours to Luxor, and 12 hours to Aswan. Sleeper cars are available on the **Overnight Luxor** and **Aswan** services.

Getting Around

Buses are slow, old and incredibly crowded. **Taxis** are cheap, but are rarely metered so fares are a matter for negotiation; if you pay more than half the driver's original asking price you are probably being ripped off. Many hotels display a list of recommended fares to specific destinations; bargaining may get you an even better deal. Sightseeing **tour coaches** are generally the easiest way of getting to Giza, Saqqara and Memphis if you don't mind being in a group.

Where to Stay

Cairo's tourist hotels cluster in three centres: on the Nile in the **Garden City** area or on the **Nile islands** in the centre; the **Heliopolis** business and residential district, northeast of the centre and close to the airport; and at **Giza**, with views of the Pyramids. Mid-range and budget hotels are found only in the city centre, with Giza and Heliopolis the domain of luxury properties and expensive hotels

City Centre

Luxury

Royal Nile Towers, Cornish el-Nil, Roda, tel: (02) 362-1717, fax: (02) 362-1927. Luxurious modern hotel.

Semiramis Inter-Continental Cairo, Cornish el-Nil, tel: (02) 795-7171, fax: (02) 796-3020. Luxury chain hotel, superb Nile views. Central.

Mid-Range/Budget

Shepheard's Hotel, Cornish el-Nil, tel: (02) 795-3801, fax: (02) 792-1010. Built in the 1950s, this five-star hotel's name is its only connection with its grand 19th-century predecessor, burnt down by rioters in 1952.

Odeon Palace Hotel, 6 Sharia Abd el-Hamid Said, Sharia Talaat Harb, tel and fax: (02) 577-6637. Affordable and central, with noisy 24-hour bar-restaurant on roof terrace.

Cairo at a Glance

Heliopolis

Luxury

Meridien Heliopolis, 51 Al Orouba Street, Heliopolis, tel: (02) 290-5055, fax: (02) 291-8591. Attractive deluxe property in landscaped gardens, sister to the Meridien Cairo.
Concorde el Salam, Abd el-Hamid Badawy, Heliopolis, tel: (02) 622-4000, fax: (02) 622-6037. Luxurious business hotel under Swiss management.

Giza

Luxury

Mena House Oberoi, Sharia al-Ahram, Giza, tel: (02) 383-3444, fax: (02) 383-7777. Superb historic hotel near the Pyramids.
Meridien Pyramids, Alexandra Desert Hotel, Giza, tel: (02) 383-0383, fax: (02) 383-1730.

Where to Eat

Most of Cairo's best restaurants are in the major hotels, though more adventurous visitors will find a choice of places to eat in all price brackets in the city centre, especially around the **Sharia Talaat Harb** area. **Heliopolis** and **Giza** have a dearth of mid-range and cheap places to eat. As with hotels, not all restaurants have fax lines.
Justine, 4 Sharia Hassan Sabri, tel: (02) 736-2961. Pompous surroundings, high prices, excellent food.
La Bodega, 26th of July Street, Zamalek, tel: (02) 735-6761. High quality, reasonably priced fusion cuisine.
La Chesa, 21 Sharia Adli, tel: (02) 393-9360. Swiss managed, clean and neat. For tourists with plain taste.
Felfela, 15 Sharia Hoda Sharawi, Sharia Talaat Harb, no telephone or fax. Egyptian food in all its forms.

Shopping

Cairo's **Khan el-Khalili bazaar** area has fantastic shopping for those prepared to bargain hard. Best buys include antique brassware, alabaster work, glassware, rugs and other textiles, and inlaid or carved woodwork. Beware of shoddy workmanship and imitation antiques; if you are offered 'antique' scarabs, papyrus paintings, or coins they are invariably fakes. If you do not wish to haggle, you can buy craftwork and reproduction antiques in the **souvenir stores** of every large hotel. Excellent, certified reproductions of archaeological finds are also sold in the official shop of the **Egyptian Antiquities Museum**.

Tours and Excursions

Misr Travel, the official Egyptian Tourist Authority Travel agency, tel and fax: (02) 684-6971, arranges a variety of sightseeing tours, travel and accommodation throughout Egypt and has branches in most tourist hotels. Some of the popular tours include guided excursions to Giza, Saqqara and Memphis, half-day visits to the Egyptian Antiquities Museum, night-time visits to the Sound and Light performances at the Pyramids of Giza, and half- or full-day Nile cruises.

Useful Contacts

Egyptian Tourist Authority Headquarters, Misr Travel Tower, Abbassia Square, Cairo, tel and fax: (02) 684-6971. Tourist information.
ETA Tourist Information offices, 5 Sharia Adli, tel: (02) 391-3454, no fax; Pyramids, tel: (02) 383-8823, no fax; Airport, tel: (02) 265-4760; Central Station, tel: (02) 579-0767. Free information brochures, maps and information on travel throughout Egypt.

CAIRO	J	F	M	A	M	J	J	A	S	O	N	D
AVERAGE TEMP. °F	66	70	75	82.5	89.5	95	95	95	91.5	86	79	70
AVERAGE TEMP. °C	19	21	24	28	32	35	35	35	33	30	26	21
HOURS OF SUN DAILY	6	7	8	9	11	12	12	12	12	11	10	8
RAINFALL in	0.25	0.2	0.16	0.12	0.12	0	0	0	0	0.16	0.2	0.25
RAINFALL mm	5	4	3	2	2	0	0	0	0	3	4	5
DAYS OF RAINFALL	3	2	1	1	1	0	0	0	0	1	1	2

EGYBEL

3
Alexandria and the Nile Delta

Between Cairo and the Mediterranean coast lies the most populous part of Egypt. Watered and fertilized by the two branches of the Nile as they fan out towards the sea, the lush farmland of the Delta has been, agriculturally, the richest part of the country since antiquity. But the life-giving Nile has also helped to erase the Delta's past. Mud brick was the most commonly used building material in Pharaonic and medieval times, as it is in Delta towns and villages today, and many of the ancient cities, tombs and temples of the Delta region have lapsed back into the mud from which they were built. Archaeologists believe there may be much still to be discovered beneath the swamps and silt of the Delta, but the waterlogged terrain does not lend itself easily to archaeological exploration.

The **Delta region** offers the visitor a window into the near-timeless world of the Egyptian *fellahin* (peasantry), whose agriculture-based way of life has changed little, and the Delta towns are known for their spectacularly colourful *mulids* (festivals) honouring Muslim holy men and women and marking the key dates of the Islamic calendar.

Alexandria, at the western edge of the Delta, is a bustling city of some five million people. Egypt's second city and its major seaport, Alexandria retains faint echoes of its former glories. Founded by Alexander the Great in the 4th century BC, it flourished as one of the greatest Graeco-Roman cities of its time and today it remains one of the most important ports of the Mediterranean.

Don't Miss

*** **Kom el-Dikka:** restored Roman theatre, the only one in Egypt.
*** **Wadi Natrun:** rich concentration of early Coptic monasteries.
** **El-Alamein:** battlefield and cemeteries mark World War II turning point.
** **Graeco-Roman Museum:** interesting insight into often-ignored era in Egypt's history.
* **Pompey's Pillar:** Roman column rising amid the bustle of the city traffic.
* **Catacombs:** eerie graves from the 2nd century BC.

Opposite: *The Cornish, Alexandria's Mediterranean waterfront.*

ALEXANDRIA CLIMATE

Alexandria's climate is characterized as Mediterranean: warm and damp in winter, hot and sunny in summer, pleasant year-round. It has the wettest microclimate in Egypt, but rain is unlikely except February–April.

Right: *Qaytbay's Fortress, the 15th-century Mameluke castle, guards the harbour.*
Opposite: *The Roman amphitheatre at Kom el-Dikka could seat up to 800 spectators.*

ALEXANDRIA

Until the second half of the 20th century, Alexandria was home to a large Greek community as well as substantial Jewish, French and Italian minorities. The majority of these people were involved in the commerce and industry sectors, and left Egypt in the 1950s because of the nationalizing policies of **Nasser**. As a result, Alexandria today, with a population of approximately three million, is far less cosmopolitan and more Egyptian than at any other time in its long history.

The historic centre of Alexandria is around the western and eastern harbours, which are separated by a promontory on which stand a **Mameluke fortress** (now a naval museum) built on the site of the famous Pharos, and a 19th-century **royal palace** (which is not open to the public). The modern-day city stretches for some 16km (10 miles) along the coast of the Mediterranean, hemmed in to the south by the **El-Mahmudiya Canal** and the brackish waters of **Lake Maryut** (Mareotis).

Qaytbay's Fortress (Naval Museum) *

North pier, Eastern Harbour. This 15th-century Mameluke castle with its round towers and battlements dominates the Eastern Harbour, where a fleet of gaily coloured wooden fishing boats is anchored. Now a naval museum, it contains charts, model ships and uniforms, as well as relics of Roman and Napoleonic sea battles. The fortress was built on the site of Pharos, the great lighthouse of Alexandria which was one of the Seven Wonders of the ancient world. The fortress was built in the 15th century, using some rubble from the ruins of **Pharos**. Open 09:00–16:00, closed Friday 12:00–13:00.

The Great Lighthouse

The **Pharos** (lighthouse) was built in 280BC by **Ptolemy II Philadelphos**. The beacon of the150m (492ft) tower, crowned by a statue of **Poseidon**, could apparently be seen for a vast distance out to sea, which indicates that the Alexandrians may have known of the lens or the mirror, as used in modern lighthouses.

Necropolis of Anfushi *

Sharia Ras el-Tin. Frescoes in these five rock tombs, discovered early this century, give a revealing glimpse into life in the Ptolemaic period. The tombs, cut in the 2nd century BC, blend Greek, Roman and Egyptian influences. Open 09:00–16:00, closed Friday 12:00–13:00.

Underwater Finds

Archaeologists using satellite imaging have discovered the ruins of **Cleopatra's Alexandria** 6m (20ft) down under the water of the modern harbour. Alexandria was inundated by an earthquake and tidal wave in AD365. One find is the wreck of a **ship** (believed to be Cleopatra's personal vessel) within the Queen's private harbour. A 374kg (825lb) **sphinx** with the face of Cleopatra's father, Ptolemy XII, and a 250kg (550lb) **statue** of a priest of Osiris were brought to the surface in October 1998.

Mosque of Abu Abbas el-Mursi **

Sharia 26 July (el-Cornish). An elegant example of Muslim religious architecture and one of Alexandria's foremost religious buildings. The original mosque was built in 1767 and named after a 13th-century Muslim cleric, **Abu Abbas el-Mursi**, whose tomb is within. Open Sunday–Thursday, men only. Dress modestly.

Kom el-Dikka (Roman Ampitheatre) ***

Midan el-Gumhuriya/ Sharia el-Horreya. This **Roman amphitheatre** has tiers of seats and a stage with a mosaic floor. Next to it are Roman baths and the newly discovered Villa of the Birds, a Roman house with beautiful mosaic floors. Open 09:00–16:00, closed Friday 12:00–13:00.

Library of Alexandria

The Great Library of Alexandria, inaugurated by Ptolemy I, was an important centre of learning. It contained 700,000 volumes, but all were lost when the library burned in the 3rd century AD. In 2002, the spectacular new Bibliotheca Alexandrina was opened. It aims to house and restore manuscripts and rare books from Egypt, the Arab world and the Mediterranean countries.

Above: *Statue of the sacred bull of Apis in the Graeco-Roman Museum.* **Below:** *Pompey's Pillar and a sphinx of the Ptolemaic era.*

Graeco-Roman Museum **

This museum is situated at the corner of Sharia el-Mathaf and Sharia el-Horreya. It contains quite a large collection of interesting finds from the Ptolemaic and Roman era, including several statues, coins and pottery figurines. Some of the high points of the exhibition include a really magnificent black granite sculpture of an **Apis bull**, a fine collection of mummies from the local tombs, and also busts of **Mark Anthony** and **Cleopatra**. The museum is open 09:00–16:00 every day, closed 11:30–13:30 on Fridays.

Pompey's Pillar (Diocletian's Column) *

Sharia Amud el-Sawari. This column was placed here to mark the victories of the 3rd-century AD Roman Emperor **Diocletian**. Its popular name is a misnomer given by medieval crusaders. Two grimy sphinxes from the Ptolemaic era are placed at its base. The column stands amidst the ruins of the Serapeum and what was once Cleopatra's library.

Kom el-Shougafa (Catacombs) **

The eerie remnants of a rather decadent mixed culture, these 2nd-century BC tombs are built around a central funerary court. Within the three levels of the tomb chambers are friezes and peculiar statues, including Medusa heads, bearded serpents and the jackal-headed **Anubis** in Roman military armour.

East of Alexandria

Alexandria's **beach strip** begins just east of the Eastern Harbour and continues eastward almost uninterrupted as far as the bourgeois suburbs of Montazah and Ma'mura. Despite this long strip of sand, Alexandria is not a great beach destination, as its town beaches suffer from urban and industrial pollution and overbuilding, as well as overcrowding and a lack of shade in summer. The most appealing beach to visitors is **Montazah**. **Ma'mura**, 1km (0.5 mile) further east, is another good bet.

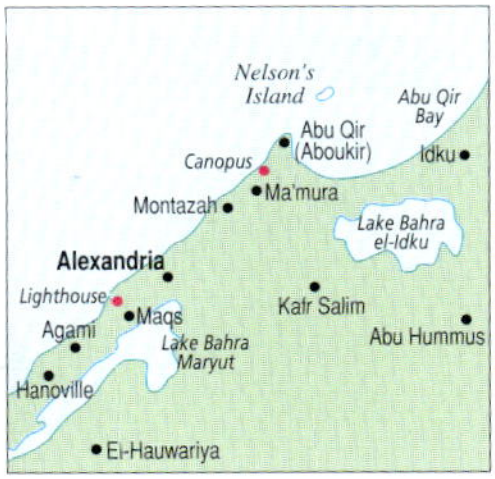

El-Montazah Palace *

Mandara/Montazah, 16km (10 miles) east of city centre. This overdone pile of florid architecture was built for the **Khedive Ismail II** and was the summer palace of the royal family, who retreated to Alexandria to escape the heat of Cairo. The park and gardens, 150 hectares (370 acres) in extent, are a popular picnic spot for Alexandrians, and there are beaches either side of the headland on which the palace stands, at Mandara (to the west) and Montazah (to the east). The building is closed, but the park is open 24 hours.

Cleopatra

Cleopatra VII Ptolemy used her exotic charms to make Egypt an ally of Rome, rather than just a conquered territory. After Julius Caesar was assassinated she managed to wrap his general, **Mark Anthony**, around her little finger. Egypt then became caught up in the war between Anthony and his rival for control of Rome, **Octavian**. Octavian defeated the fleets of Anthony and Cleopatra off the Greek coast at Actium in 30BC. Anthony committed suicide and Cleopatra killed herself by the venomous bite of a pet asp.

Aboukir (Abu Qir) *

This small seaside town 24km (15 miles) east of Alexandria is virtually a suburb of the larger city and is a popular day-trip destination for Alexandrians, who travel here to dine at its waterfront seafood restaurants. Two great battles of the **Napoleonic War** were fought here; just offshore, at the battle of Aboukir Bay (also known as the Battle of the Nile), the British Admiral Horatio Nelson sank Napoleon's fleet in 1798, stranding the French expeditionary force in Egypt. The following year, Bonaparte's army of occupation defeated a 15,000-strong Turkish force, sent in by the British, which had landed at Aboukir in an attempt to drive out the French invaders.

Below: *The new Bibliotheca Alexandrina aims to continue Alexandria's ancient tradition of learning.*

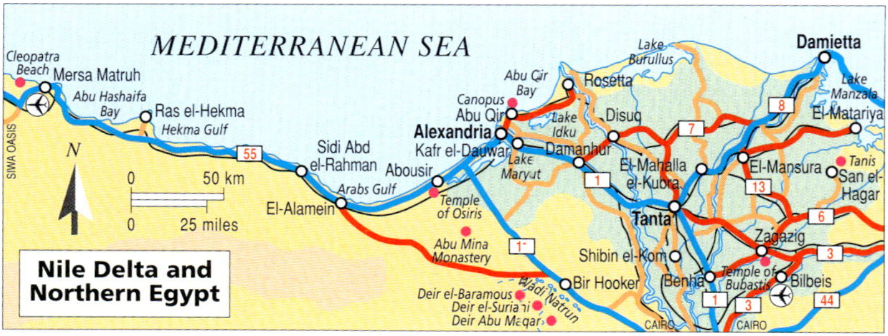

> **ROMAN CHAMELEONS?**
>
> Herpetologists recently discovered an isolated population of African chameleons living wild in the marshes outside Alexandria. Individuals are larger and are a different colour from those living south of the Sahara, and may even be a new species. Even more surprisingly, a similar population has been found at Pylos, in southern Greece – another Roman settlement which was once on the sea route between Alexandria and Rome. The Romans in Egypt are known to have kept chameleons as pets, and there is speculation that these two populations may be their descendants.

Canopus *

A dilapidated Mameluke fort stands on the site of the Ptolemaic city of Canopus. The remnants of this settlement, which flourished before Alexandria developed, include the foundations of a **Temple of Serapis**. Artefacts from this site can be seen in the **Graeco-Roman Museum** in Alexandria. Open 09:00–16:00.

The Mediterranean coast stretches eastwards from here in a great sweep, broken by the mouths of the Nile and by a few small ports, and often backed by lagoons and salt marshes which make the coast a haven for migrating waterfowl. This area of Egypt is little visited, though its stretches of sandy seashore are unlikely to escape attention forever. Along the coast, some low-scale development has taken place, attracting a mainly Egyptian and Middle Eastern clientele in summer, when Cairenes and other city dwellers make every effort to escape the heat.

Right: *Fishing boats seen against the backdrop of high-rises at Alexandria.*
Opposite: *A multitude of graves populate a war cemetery at El-Alamein.*

West of Alexandria

An excellent coastal highway runs parallel to the Mediterranean as far as the Libyan border and beyond. Crossing to Libya is open to foreigners with a valid visa in advance. About 45km (28 miles) west of Alexandria is the town of **Abousir** (Abu Sir), not to be confused with Abousir at Giza. This undistinguished small town was in ancient times named Taposiris and a few ruins remain.

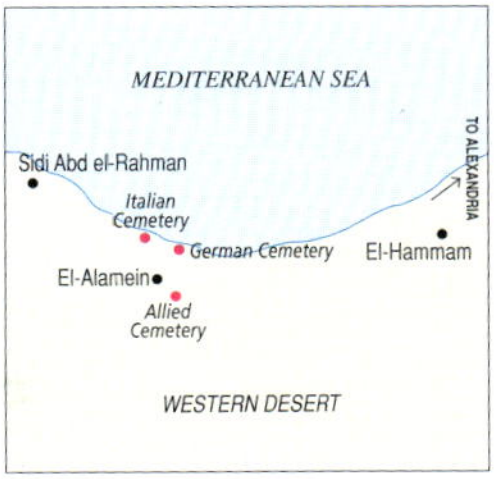

Temple of Osiris **

This is one of the few unprotected and almost unvisited ancient temples in Egypt, offering you the rare chance to scramble to the top of its walls for views of the desert, the coastline, and Lake Maryut. The temple dates from the Hellenistic era, as does the stone lighthouse tower next to the temple, said to be a smaller model of the famous Pharos lighthouse at Alexandria.

El-Alamein

The battle of El-Alamein was the culmination of a three-year campaign in the Western Desert, with the Allies first repelling an Italian assault and then in turn being rolled back by Rommel's Afrika Korps. Rommel's forces ran out of steam only 100km (62 miles) from Alexandria and were decisively defeated by the Allied army which outnumbered Rommel's tanks, artillery and infantry and had near-total control of the air.

El-Alamein **

This is the site of two of the most decisive battles of the 20th century, when Allied troops first (in July 1942) checked the Axis forces in their headlong advance on Alexandria, then (in October–November 1942) forced them onto the retreat after a 12-day battle. El-Alamein village is of little interest, and the almost featureless desert battlefield itself is of interest only to serious military historians, but the **museum** and **cemeteries** nearby are worth a visit in passing. There are fine sandy beaches on the coast here, but they have few if any facilities and are often windswept and extremely hot.

El-Alamein Museum **

Battered war machines of the German, Italian and British forces, including tanks, armoured cars, field pieces and mobile guns, stand on plinths at this museum, preserved despite their age by the dry desert air. Worth seeing for anyone with an interest in **military history**. Open 09:00–18:00, during Ramadan 09:00–15:00.

Popsky's Private Army

One of the more colourful characters of the desert war was **Vladimir Poliakoff**, an Anglophile Belgian of Russian descent. The chief engineer on a sugar-cane plantation, Poliakoff explored the desert in his spare time, navigating by stars and sextant. In his 40s when war broke out, he was deemed too old for anything but a desk job, but by stubbornness and intrigue he created a virtually independent mobile fighting force of British, South African, Australian and New Zealand volunteers which struck deep behind enemy lines to sabotage fuel and ammunition depots, attack airfields and, on at least one occasion, organize mass escapes of Allied prisoners of war.

Allied War Cemetery **

This moving, simple memorial to the thousands of British and Commonwealth soldiers and Allied troops who died at El-Alamein is situated approximately 500m (550yd) to the east of the village. It is a reminder that Montgomery's 8th Army was made up not only of British soldiers but also of recruits from Australia and New Zealand, both black and white Africans, Gurkhas and Indians – many of whom are buried here in the desert. Further to the west are the Italian and German War Cemeteries. Only serious war buffs will find a reason to visit either of these graveyards. The cemeteries are open 09:00–18:00 daily.

Mersa Matruh *

Much fought-over during World War II, Mersa Matruh is a modern town built on the site of Roman Paraetonium, 300km (180 miles) west of Alexandria on the coastal highway. It has beautiful white beaches (like Alexandria's they are overcrowded in summer, while most hotels are closed in winter), but few sights of real interest, and is mostly visited as a stopping-off point en route from Alexandria to the desert oasis of **Siwa** (see the Western Desert Oases, page 120).

Cleopatra Beach (Cleopatra's Bath) *

Several natural rock pools near Mersa Matruh are claimed as the favoured bathing spot of the last Queen of Egypt. The nearest, 1km (0.5 mile) north of town, is a pleasant place for a dip if you want to cool off after a desert drive.

Left: *Bringing in the harvest in the farmlands of the Nile Delta.*
Opposite: *The scenic Mediterranean shore at Mersa Matruh.*

The Nile Delta

The Delta is a picturesque region to journey through and with its mud-brick villages often painted in bright hues of blue, green or yellow, its radiantly verdant fields of sugar cane and cotton, its sailing boats and ox carts, it is a rich source of photogenic images for the camera or video recorder. However, the Delta region is less richly endowed with spectacular sights than other parts of the country. The Delta provinces are among the least-visited parts of Egypt, and have few amenities designed for foreign travellers. No one sight stands out as worthy of visiting on its own, but there is enough to see in the region to make a multi-centre journey by bus, train or taxi worthwhile for the more adventurous traveller. The best jumping-off point for a Delta tour is the city of **Zagazig**, about 80km (50 miles) northeast of Cairo and the biggest of the southern Delta towns.

Temple of Bubastis ★

Not surprisingly, the temple which was dedicated to the goddess **Bastet** – one of the most ancient temples in the region – is also one of the most ruined. It dates from the Old Kingdom, but was reconstructed by the Pharaohs of the 22nd Dynasty, who made their capital at Tanis in the Delta. Situated approximately 3km (2 miles) south of Zagazig on the Bilbeis road, the temple is open 09:00–16:00 every day.

The Shadouf

Travellers in the Delta may still see in use today one of the oldest Egyptian devices, the shadouf (sometimes called the 'Egyptian water-wheel'). First depicted in paintings and carvings of the 19th Dynasty (1300–1200BC), the shadouf is no more than a bucket or pot suspended over a river or irrigation canal from the long end of a counterpoised pole. The bucket is filled from the water source, then the weight of the counterpoise – a boulder or a block of concrete – hoists it to the level of the bank, where the water is emptied into channels leading it to the area to be irrigated. The process consumes much more time and labour than a real water-wheel, but time and manpower have never been in short supply in Egypt.

Above: *The mulids are the most colourful events in the Nile Delta.*
Opposite: *Coptic Monks at one of the monasteries of Wadi Natrun.*

Tanis *

The ruins of the ancient city of Tanis lie near the village of San el-Hagar, 75km (47 miles) northeast of Zagazig. The temple enclosure of the **Temple of Amun** surrounds toppled colossi and cavernous tombs of Pharaohs of the 21st and 22nd Dynasties, who made their royal seat here. Magnificent relics from the tombs, recovered during the 19th century, can be seen at the Egyptian Antiquities Museum in Cairo. Open 09:00–16:00.

Damietta (Dumyat) *

Near the Mediterranean, 125km (70 miles) northeast of Zagazig, is a river port on the eastern arm of the Nile which in medieval times exported Delta cotton to Europe, giving its name to the fabric known as **'dimity'**. East of Damietta is Lake Manzala, a vast expanse of reed beds and brackish waters cut off from the sea by a strip of scrubland and dunes, and a good place to see Egypt's birdlife.

OMM KOLTHUM

The voice you hear singing plaintive Egyptian songs over your hotel sound system, on the radio, or on the cassette deck of your coach or taxi is as likely as not to be that of Omm Kolthum. Though she died in 1975, the Egyptian singer shaped modern Arab music not just in Egypt but across the Arab world. She came on the scene at a time when Egypt was being reshaped, and is still very much perceived as one of the voices of the Egyptian people.

Tanta **

Dull and grimy most of the year, Tanta springs to life in October for the annual autumn *mulid* (festival) celebrating the harvesting of the cotton crop. Attended by hundreds of thousands of Egyptians, these part-religious, part-secular celebrations can be fascinating and intense experiences.

Rosetta (Rashid) *

Rosetta, about 90km (60 miles) north of Tanta, re-entered history with the discovery of the Rosetta Stone in 1799. Substantial merchants' mansions dating from the 17th and 18th centuries, when Rosetta became Egypt's main Mediterranean seaport, can still be seen on the streets of this quiet, commercial centre built around a fishing harbour. Some 15km (10 miles) to the east is **Lake Burullus**, a brackish lagoon. The lake opens onto the Mediterranean and provides rich fishing grounds and habitats for wildfowl.

Wadi Natrun

Beyond the fringes of the Delta, and separated from it by a strip of desert 20km (12 miles) wide, Wadi Natrun is just off the **Desert Highway**, close to the village of Bir Hooker. A relatively fertile area in the desert, Wadi Natrun is one of the remaining heartlands of Coptic Christianity and has some of the oldest **monasteries** in the world, some of them dating from the 4th century AD, though all have been extensively rebuilt over the centuries. Protected by their relative isolation, the monasteries were also defended against Bedouin attackers by huge fortress walls.

Photography

If you are using a **specialist film**, take a plentiful supply. Only standard print brands are readily available in Egypt and may have been stored in less than optimum conditions. Processing in Egypt is not always reliable. For best results, take pictures first thing in the morning or late afternoon. A slow film will produce rich colour saturation. Note that use of flash is banned in most tombs and museums. Attendants may offer to turn a blind eye for baksheesh, but you should resist the temptation.

Deir el-Suriani ***

About 7km (4 miles) southwest of Bir Hooker. With its elaborate domes, spires and crucifixes, Deir el-Suriani, the most remarkable of Wadi Natrun's monasteries, is as lavishly adorned within as it is externally. Inside, the 10th-century chapel of **el-Adra** (the Virgin Mary) has frescoes of the Nativity and the Annunciation. Open 10:00–17:00.

Deir el-Baramous**

Some 12km (7.5 miles) northwest of Bir Hooker. Walls more than 10m (30ft) high surround this 9th-century monastery. The oldest surviving sections are the refectory, where monks still eat, and caves in the cliffs nearby once provided refuge for Coptic hermits. Open 10:00–17:00.

Deir Abu Maqar **

About 13km (8 miles) south of Bir Hooker. Much new building has not eradicated the character of this thriving monastery with its domed church of St John and apocalyptic frescoes, monastery church of St Macarius and battlemented inner keep dating from the 11th century.

Alexandria and the Nile Delta at a Glance

Best Times To Visit

Spring and **early summer** (April–June) and **autumn** (September–October) are the best times to visit, though the Mediterranean coast is pleasant in high summer too for those who enjoy really hot weather. The coast is often wet and windswept in winter.

Getting There

International flights from some European and most Middle East cities; internal flights from Cairo. A new international airport has been built near Borg el-Arab on a site 26km (16 miles) from Alexandria. Opened in 2001, the airport is expected to make Alexandria more accessible to and popular with European visitors, offering more direct scheduled and charter flights from Europe.

Two **highways** connect Alexandria with Cairo; the older of the two cuts through the Nile Delta, passing through Tanta, while a newer, faster highway skirts the Delta and runs southeast through the desert to enter Cairo through Giza.

A coastal highway runs westward, connecting Alexandria with the Libyan border. Express buses run on all these highways.

The **railway** runs through the Delta from Cairo to Alexandria via Tanta, an attractive scenic trip.

Getting Around

Taxis are quite cheap, and for tourists they are the best way of getting around, but alternatives include **trams** (some of which have one carriage reserved exclusively for women), **buses** and also incredibly crowded **minibuses**. The central tram terminus is Ramla Station.

Where to Stay

The only luxury and mid-range hotels in the region are in Alexandria and the coastal resorts. Four- and five-star hotels around Alexandria are along the **Mediterranean seafront** and clustered at **Montazah**. Cheaper hotels are central. Accommodation in the Delta towns is extremely basic and not recommended.

Alexandria

Luxury

Hilton Borg el-Arab Resort, Kilometre 52, Alexandria-Matruh Road, North Coast, tel: (03) 374-0740, fax: (03) 374-0760. New five-star luxury resort opened in 1999 in the purpose-built resort suburb of Borg el-Arab. Facilities include 167 rooms and 80 sea-view chalets, private beach, pool, watersports, health club, tennis court, children's club and landscaped gardens. Two restaurants offer Mediterranean and gourmet cuisine.

El-Salamlek Palace Hotel, Montazah, Alexandria, PO Box 258, tel: (03) 547-7999, fax: (03) 547-3585. The most characterful and picturesque hotel in Alexandria, with 20 rooms set in the gardens of the Montazah Palace.

Cecil Hotel, Midan Sa'ad Zaghloul, tel: (03) 484-0367, fax: (03) 485-5655. Old-fashioned grand hotel overlooking the Eastern Harbour.

Sheraton Montazah, Sharia Abu Qir, tel: (03) 548-0550, fax: (03) 540-1331. Modern luxury hotel with sea views, opposite Montazah Palace.

Helnan Palestine Hotel, Montazah Palace Complex, tel: (03) 547-3500, fax: (03) 547-3378. Pleasant hotel in palace grounds, overlooking the beach.

Mid-Range

Mamoura Palace Hotel, tel and fax: (03) 547-3450, or (03) 547-3383. Set back from the beach, small garden.

Metropole Hotel, Sharia Sa'ad Zaghloul, tel: (03) 486-1465, fax: (03) 486-2040. Moderate and central with old-fashioned style and sea views.

El-Alamein

El-Alamein Hotel, Alamein Beach, tel: (046) 468-0140, fax: (046) 468-0341. This is the only hotel in El-Alamein.

Mersa Matruh

Luxury

Hotel Beau Site, Sharia el-Cornish, tel: (046) 493-2066,

Alexandria and the Nile Delta at a Glance

fax: (046) 493-3319. On the beach with sea views.

Mid-Range

Negresco Hotel, tel: (046) 493-4492, fax: (046) 493-3960. Another waterfront hotel, clean and well priced.

Budget

Miami Hotel, corner of Sharia el-Cornish and Sharia Zaher Galal, tel: (046) 493-4810, fax: (046) 493-2083. Large three-star close to town centre.

Where to Eat

Alexandria has a wide range of places to eat and some excellent fish restaurants. In other towns, the choice is between nameless snack stands and hotel restaurants.

Alexandria

If in doubt, head for **Sharia Safiya Zaghloul**, lined with restaurants in every category.

El-Ekhlass, 49 Sharia Safiya Zaghloul, tel: (03) 486-4434, no fax. Superb Egyptian cooking, traditional dishes.

Santa Lucia, 40 Sharia Safiya Zaghloul, tel: (03) 486-0332, no fax. Good choice for freshly caught, well-prepared seafood.

L'Ossobucco, 14 El-Horreya Ave, tel: (03) 487-8082. Mid-range Italian restaurant.

Chez Gaby, 22 El-Horreya Ave, tel: (03) 487-4306. Egyptian-influenced French restaurant.

Denis, 1 Ibn Bassaam, Ramla Station, tel: (03) 486-1709. Conveniently located fish restaurant.

Pastroudis, 39 Gamel Abdel Nasser, El-Horreya, tel: (03) 492-9609. Greek restaurant.

Hassan Bleik, 18 Sharia Sa'ad Zaghloul. Fine Lebanese food.

Aboukir

Aboukir is noted for **seafood**, and Alexandrians travel from town to eat here. Few restaurants have faxes, and some do not have telephones. Walk along the waterfront after sunset and follow your nose.

El-Alamein

See Where to Stay.

Mersa Matruh

See Where to Stay.

Shopping

Flea Market, Rue Attarine, Alexandria. Wide assortment of genuine and fake antiques and bric-a-brac. You might find something original or interesting if you look hard enough; haggle fiercely if you do.

Tours and Excursions

Desert safaris, visits to the Delta sites and festivals, and tours to El-Alamein and Siwa Oasis via Mersa Matruh are best experienced as part of an escorted **package tour** organized by an international tour operator such as Holts Tours, 15 Market Street, Sandwich, Kent, CT13 9DA, UK, tel: (01304) 612-248, fax (01304) 614-930. **Local tour agencies** also offer individual and group arrangements, either by coach, minibus or chauffeur-driven car. Agencies in Alexandria include:

Misr Hanoville, 19 Sharia Sa'ad Zaghloul, tel: (03) 486-6501, fax: (03) 486-0049.

Misr Travel, 33 Salah Salim, tel: (03) 484-6001, fax: (03) 486-9617.

Thomas Cook, 15 Sharia Sa'ad Zaghloul, tel: (03) 487-5118, fax: (03) 487-4073

Chauffeur-driven cars can be rented by the day or week from **Limousine Rent Cars**, Smouha, tel: (03) 582-3721.

Useful Contacts

Tourist Office, Ramla Station, corner Midan Sa'ad Zaghloul and Sharia Nabi Daniel, tel and fax: (03) 484-3380. Open 08:00–18:00. Range of tourist information and maps, free guide to city.

Tourist Police, tel: 126. Upstairs from Tourist Office.

ALEXANDRIA	J	F	M	A	M	J	J	A	S	O	N	D
AVERAGE TEMP. °F	64.5	66	68	73.5	79	81	82.5	86	82.5	81	77	68
AVERAGE TEMP. °C	18	19	20	23	26	27	28	30	28	27	25	20
HOURS OF SUN DAILY	6	6	7	8	9	12	12	12	11	9	8	7
RAINFALL in	2	1.5	1	0.25	0	0	0	0	0.25	1	1.5	2
RAINFALL mm	50	30	20	5	0	0	0	0	5	20	30	55
DAYS OF RAINFALL	5	4	3	1	0	0	0	0	1	3	4	5

4
The Lower Nile

South of Cairo the course of the Nile meanders through desert, though the narrow band of cultivation on either bank means the traveller by rail, road or Nile cruiser sees little of the endless expanse of sand beyond the irrigated farmland. This lower stretch of the Nile is populous and rich in ancient remains dating from the Pharaonic, Roman and medieval eras in Egypt's history. Until the massacre of tourists by Islamic terrorists at Luxor in November 1997, the easiest and most popular way of seeing the sights of the Lower Nile area was by **river cruiser**, starting at either Cairo or Luxor and taking several days on the way, calling at all the main sights.

However, the riverside towns of **El-Minya** and **Asyut** and the surrounding areas have been identified as the homeland of the terrorist group which carried out the Luxor massacre and which between 1992 and 1997 conducted a campaign of violence against the Egyptian government, mainly in Minya and Asyut provinces. Most of these incidents were directed at police, or were sectarian in nature. Since the Luxor attack, the main extremist groups have publicly renounced violence, although the government is still wary, and security forces still insist that foreigners travel through the region in convoy under armed escort. River cruisers are still not operating between Luxor and Cairo, and the British Foreign Office still advises travellers to remain vigilant and to respect any advice from the local security authorities, especially when they are visiting the Nile Valley south of and including Minya Province.

Don't Miss

*** **El-Faiyum Oasis:** an oasis near the Nile with desert landscapes and old-fashioned villages.
*** **Abydos:** this stunning temple complex dates from reign of Seti I.
*** **Dendera:** mighty temple to Hathor, Roman temple and Christian basilica.
** **Deir el-Abyad:** remarkable ruined church dating from the 4th century.

Opposite: *Women carry sacks of cotton by the banks of the Nile.*

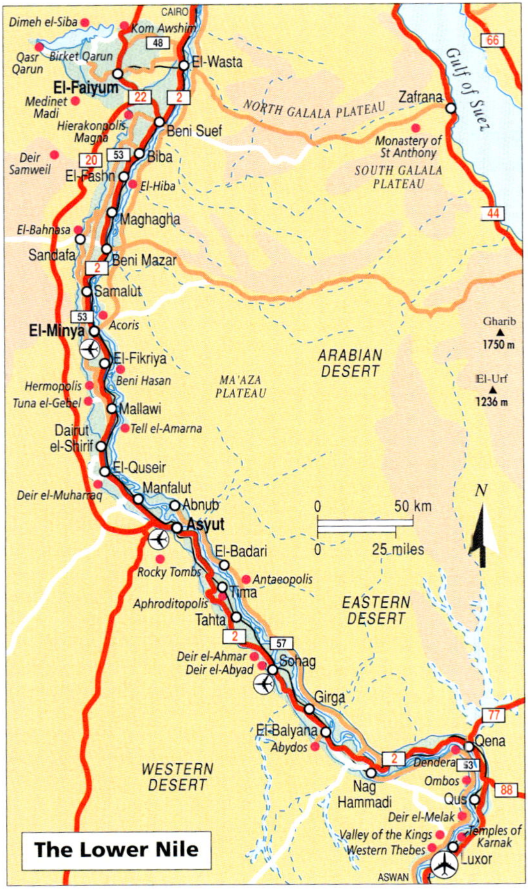

Lower Nile Climate

This region has a desert climate, with clear dry air. It is usually very hot from June to August. Winter days are warm but nights can be very chilly. Best times to visit are **spring** and **autumn**. Rain is very rare at any time of year.

El-Faiyum

Around 100km (62 miles) southwest of Cairo, the lush farmlands of the Nile bulge out into the surrounding desert, forming an enclave of greenery fed by more than 2000km (1243 miles) of irrigation channels. The Faiyum is not a new project to make the desert bloom, but has been farmed since the earliest times. It lies in a shallow depression, which makes it easy to bring water from the Nile, feeding the natural reservoir of **Birket (Lake) Qarun**, a lake of 40km (25 miles) long on the northern side of the Faiyum.

Like the Nile Delta, the lush Faiyum area is a photographer's dream, and it is also dotted with a scattering of ancient sites. More than 200 stream-driven waterwheels across the region, four of which are functioning models, still lift water from canals and wells. **Medinet el-Faiyum**, the Faiyum's commercial centre, is rather drab and uninteresting, but is the inevitable gateway to the region.

Obelisk of Senusert I ⋆

Situated on the Cairo road, unenclosed. The 13m (43ft) high column, standing on a roundabout at the entrance to town when approaching from the Cairo highway, dates from the 12th Dynasty.

Kom Awshim (Karanis) **

Highway 22, approximately 30km (19 miles) north of Medinet el-Faiyum. In late Roman times the desert encroached on the outer reaches of the Faiyum and several towns of the Ptolemaic era were abandoned to the sands. Ancient **Karanis** is the easiest to get to, and has fine views of Birket Qarun and the Faiyum. The ground layout of the ancient town and the remains of two temples can be clearly seen. There is also a **museum**, with a small collection of finds from the area. Open 09:00–16:00, closed Mondays.

SOBEK AND RENENUNET

The crocodile god **Sobek** was worshipped especially in El-Faiyum and Kom Ombo on the Nile, where the Nile crocodile (now extinct in Egypt except in Lake Nasser) was quite common in ancient times. With his elaborate crown, Sobek was one of the many symbols of royalty. **Renenunet**, a serpent goddess also much revered in El-Faiyum, was another protector of the Pharaoh.

Dimeh el-Siba (Soknopaiou Nisos) **

North shore of Birket Qarun, accessible by 4-wheel drive or by boat from the south shore, not enclosed. Like Karanis, this Ptolemaic town was also abandoned to the desert. The ruins stand about 3km (2 miles) from the lake and include the foundations of streets and houses, city walls, and a **Temple to Isis and Soknopaios**, the latter being one of the many gods invented during the Ptolemaic era.

Qasr Qarun (Dionysias) *

Situated some 50km (31 miles) northwest of Medinet el-Faiyum at the western end of Birket Qarun are the remains of the Graeco-Roman city of **Dionysias**. The ruins include a well-preserved temple to the crocodile-headed god Sobek. Open 09:00–16:00.

Medinet Madi **

About 15km (10 miles) south of Abu Gandir village, which is 20km (12 miles) southwest of Medinet el-Faiyum. Another Sobek temple, from the 12th Dynasty, stands in the desert and is approached by a processional avenue guarded by sphinxes. The maze-like, roofless ruins of the later mud-brick town stand around it and a mud-brick Ptolemaic temple has recently been discovered. The site is not enclosed.

Below: *Sphinxes guard the processional way at Medinet Madi.*

MUMMIES AT SOHAG

Among the newest Egyptian finds are the coffins and mummies discovered in 1998 at **Deir el-Abyad**, near Sohag (Lower Nile), where researchers of the Supreme Council for Antiquities have found a mountaintop tomb carved in stone and dating from 2700BC. The tomb contains the body of a man named Anny who, according to the inscriptions, was governor of the Ninth Region of Upper Egypt. The tomb also contains the wooden coffins of a man named Akkar and a woman called Ni Ankh, as well as two nameless **sarcophagi**. The five mummies are in good condition and are still covered in their original linen cloths. The site is still being researched. It is not yet open to the public, nor is it likely to be for some years.

EL-MINYA

This prosperous commercial town on the west bank, 250km (155 miles) south of Cairo, is claimed to be the heartland of Islamic fundamentalism. Advice against visiting on security grounds may be over-cautious, but there are in any case many places of greater interest to visit, and Minya is no great loss to any itinerary.

Tell el-Amarna (Akhetaten) *

Situated on the east bank of the Nile, about 68km (42 miles) to the south of El-Minya. The capital of the reforming Pharaoh **Akhenaten** (father of Tutankhamun) is a ghostly place, with very little to indicate its former glory. Tutankhamun returned his capital to Thebes on his father's death and the city subsequently fell into disuse. The treasures and relics from the cliff-face tombs above the Nile are now in the Egyptian Antiquities Museum in Cairo.

ASYUT

Some 380km (225 miles) south of Cairo, this city of 250,000 people on the Nile is a large commercial centre and was once the head of the caravan route to the Western Desert, but has no sights of note.

Deir el-Muharraq (Burnt Monastery) **

Situated 50km (31 miles) north of Asyut, west bank, on the fringe of the desert, a substantial Coptic monastery stands next to an 8th-century chapel which marks a cave where the Holy Family took refuge during their sojourn in Egypt. There are many such caves in Egypt, each venerated by Coptic Christians. The monastery also has a 12th-century keep tower. Usually open 10:00–17:00.

Deir el-Abyad (White Monastery) **

About 5km (3 miles) from the town of Sohag on the main Nile highway. This fantastic church dating from the 4th century AD is the focus of a **Christian pilgrimage and festival** in mid-July. The huge basilica stands amid the ruins of a monastery which once housed 2000 monks and is built of white limestone. There is still a small community of monks here today, and a Coptic school. Hidden in a village 4km (2.5 miles) further on, the smaller **Deir el-Ahmar** or **Red Monastery** was founded by Bishoi, a thief who converted to Christianity, and is named for the colour of the bricks used to build its outer wall. Open 07:00–18:00.

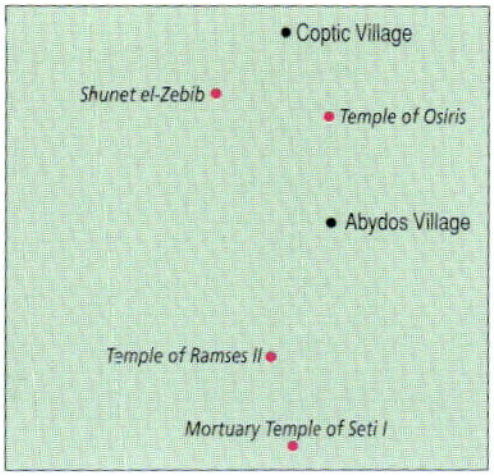

Abydos

West bank, 10km (6 miles) from El-Balyana village, 80km (50 miles) south of Sohag. The temple complex of Abydos, sacred to **Osiris**, god of the dead, is one of the most impressive ancient sites between the Cairo area and Luxor, and receives far fewer visitors than the larger temples of the Luxor area, which means it is possible to explore it at your leisure. Open 07:00–18:00.

Opposite: *The huge basilica of Deir el-Abyad, or the White Monastery.*
Below: *The impressive columns of the temple of Seti I at Abydos.*

Mortuary Temple of Seti I ***

The 19th Dynasty Pharaoh Seti I had a mortuary temple built here, and its inner hall is decorated with frescoes which include portraits of Seti I, probably from life, as they are virtually identical to the depiction of the Pharaoh on his mummy casing in the Egyptian Antiquities Museum in Cairo. The decoration of the outer hall was completed by Seti I's son and heir, Ramses II, after his death. The **cartouches** (Pharaonic seals) carved in the **Gallery of the Kings** show the line of succession from the Pharaoh Menes through his successors to Seti I.

Temple of Ramses II **

Much damaged by time and looters, the roof of this temple has collapsed and many of its columns and statues have been removed.

Temple of Osiris *

This was once the sacred hub of the **Abydos** complex, but only traces of its foundations have survived among the equally faint traces of the ancient town which stood next to the temple.

Above: *The forbidding facade of the Temple of Hathor at Dendera.*

Qena and Dendera

Situated about 64km (40 miles) north of Luxor, **Qena** is a crossroads market town surrounded by farmland where the desert road to Safaga and the Red Sea Coast connects with the Cairo–Luxor–Aswan highway. Though Qena has no sights of its own, it offers a glimpse of everyday life away from the tourist-oriented world of Luxor. Its only real interest for the traveller is as a transport hub, and as the nearest town to the temples at Dendera.

On the west bank, opposite Qena and 5km (3 miles) west of the river, **Dendera** is the single most impressive **temple complex** between Luxor and Cairo. Dendera was occupied from the earliest times, but the exceptionally well-preserved tombs, temples and statuary date from the Ptolemaic-Roman period, with depictions of Roman emperors as well as Pharaohs on the temple walls.

Temple of Hathor ***

This rectangular temple complex, 250m (820ft) long by 80m (262ft) wide, was dedicated to the goddess of beauty, pleasure, love and family, cow-headed **Hathor**, whose face crowns each of the two dozen pillars in the Outer Hypostyle Hall. Friezes depicting Roman emperors from Augustus to Nero paying homage to Hathor show that her cult survived well into the Roman era. Just south of the Temple of Hathor stands the smaller **Temple of the Birth of Isis**, built by Augustus.

Coptic Basilica *

This 5th-century Christian church is immediately to the north of the Temple of Hathor. North and south of it stand two rectangular 'birth houses', known as the **Roman Mammisi** and the **Mammisi of Nectanebo**. They were built in Roman times and dedicated to Hathor.

Black, White, or Neither?

Early European visitors, blinkered by the racism of the times, would not believe that the engineering marvels of ancient Egypt could have been built by non-Europeans. They constructed fanciful theories to explain them. But black scholars have been equally eager to claim the Egyptians as their own ancestors. The African-American writer **Edward Wilmot Blyden**, who visited Egypt in 1866, wrote of his great sense of racial pride on first seeing the Pyramids: 'I felt that I had a peculiar heritage in the Great Pyramid built by the enterprising sons of Ham, from which I descended...'. Meanwhile the Senegalese historian **Cheikh Anta Diop** theorized that Egypt was the cradle of a black African civilization that was taken over by the ancient Greeks.

Lower Nile at a Glance

Best Times To Visit

Pleasant in **winter** and **spring** (November–April), with warm days and cool, even chilly, nights. From June to September the area is unpleasantly hot. **Rain** is rare.

Getting There

Nile **cruise ships** were not operating between Cairo and Luxor at time of writing. **El-Faiyum** in the north is most conveniently reached from Cairo, whereas **Abydos** and **Dendera** are most easily reached from Luxor. **Buses** connect **Medinet el-Faiyum** with Cairo via Highway 22. Faiyum is located about 40km (25 miles) west of Beni Suef. **Highway 2** runs along the Nile from Cairo to Luxor and on to Aswan. Express coach services connect all Nile towns with Cairo and Luxor. Armed police escort some services. **Highway 77** runs between Qena and Safaga on the Red Sea and express buses operate between Qena, Safaga and Hurghada. Foreign visitors may be required to travel in an escorted convoy on these routes for security reasons. **Shared taxis** run between towns but are often unwilling to carry foreigners. Armed police checkpoints are frequent, and entire towns may be closed to foreign visitors at any time. **Trains** run between Cairo and all the towns of the lower Nile region.

Getting Around

In the towns transport options include **taxis**, **minibuses** and **horse-drawn carriages** (*caleches* or *hantours*). In view of the security situation, visitors are sometimes restricted to travelling in escorted sightseeing coaches operated by tour agencies such as Misr Travel or Isis Travel. Shared taxis operate around the Faiyum region; taxis are an alternative option even for longer journeys.

Where to Stay

El-Faiyum Oasis

Luxury

Auberge du Lac, Shakshuk, south side of Birket Qarun, tel and fax: (084) 830-730. An atmospheric four-star on the lake, this was once King Farouk's private shooting lodge.

Mid-Range

Panorama Shakshuk Hotel, Shakshuk, near Auberge du Lac, tel and fax: (084) 830-746, or (084) 830-757. Just as good a location as that of Auberge du Lac, but has cheaper rates.

Lower Nile Towns

Accommodation limited, with few acceptable hotels. For visits to Dendera and Abydos, base yourself at Luxor (see Luxor At a Glance page 90).

Tours and Excursions

Because of the threat posed by fundamentalist terrorist groups, there were no tours or excursions originating in the Lower Nile region when this book was researched, and cruises on the Lower Nile between Luxor and Cairo were suspended. International package tour companies currently steer clear of the region on government advice. Consult the latest advisories from the **UK Foreign and Commonwealth Office**, the **US State Department** or your own government before travelling independently in this area.

Useful Contacts

Medinet el-Faiyum

Tourist Office, Governorate Building, Sharia Sa'ad Zaghloul, tel: (084) 342-313. Open daily 09:00–17:00, closed Friday.

Asyut

Tourist Office, 1st Floor, Governorate Building, Sharia al Thawra, tel: (088) 310-010. Open daily 09:00–17:00, closed Friday.

LOWER NILE	J	F	M	A	M	J	J	A	S	O	N	D
AVERAGE TEMP. °F	55.5	61	64.5	68	79	82.5	86	86	82.5	75	66	59
AVERAGE TEMP. °C	13	16	18	20	26	28	30	30	28	24	19	15
HOURS OF SUN DAILY	6	7	8	9	11	12	12	12	12	11	10	8
RAINFALL	0	0	0	0	0	0	0	0	0	0	0	0

5
Luxor and Surrounds

Known to the ancient Greeks as Thebes and to the later Arabs as **El-Uqsur** ('the palaces'), the tombs, colossal statues and temples of the Luxor area are unchallenged as by far the most fascinating collection of ancient relics in Egypt. The impact on the visitor of the enormous temple complex at **Karnak**, the statues and sphinxes of the **Temple of Luxor**, and the eerie tomb chambers of the **Valley of the Kings** is even greater than that of the Sphinx and the Pyramids, and whereas the sights of Cairo have to contend with the concrete and asphalt tide of the modern city, those of Luxor stand in magnificent isolation. In fact, so rich is the Luxor region in antiquities that some of its relics, which would rate as top sights to see elsewhere, fade almost into insignificance in this crowded context.

Modern Luxor is a pleasant, small city on the east bank of the Nile and depends almost entirely on tourism, with white-sailed *feluccas* for hire on the silver waters of the Nile and brightly coloured *caleches* (open horse-drawn carriages) with white-turbaned drivers clip-clopping along the riverside **Cornish el-Nil**. Palm trees line the riverside and brightly coloured minarets surround the **Temple of Luxor**, in the centre of town.

The vast **Karnak** – the largest temple complex in the world – stands on the northern edge of Luxor. Across the river, the **Valleys of the Kings**, **Queens** and **Nobles**, the **Temple of Hatshepsut**, the **Ramesseum** and a scattering of other relics stand on the fringe of the cultivated area and amid savage, arid mountain scenery.

Don't Miss

*** **Luxor Temple:** superb temple with colossal statues and processional avenue.
*** **Temple of Karnak:** world's largest temple complex, utterly fascinating.
*** **Valley of the Kings:** tombs of the greatest of all the Pharaohs.
*** **Valley of the Queens:** burial site of ancient queens, princes and princesses.
*** **Tombs of the Nobles:** smaller, more intimate tombs of the priestly caste.

Opposite: *Seated colossi guard the entrance to the Temple of Luxor.*

> **Luxor Climate**
>
> Luxor has a typical desert climate, which is very pleasant during the **winter** months, although it can become quite cold at night. It is very hot in summer (June–September) and at the height of summer temperatures above 40°C (104°F) are common. **Rain** hardly ever falls here.

Right: *A dramatic sunset on the Nile at Luxor.*
Opposite: *Crouching sphinxes along the processional avenue at Luxor.*

Luxor

Though Luxor is a major hub of tourism, village life continues almost untouched by tourism in the villages around it. The town is surrounded by sugar-cane and alfalfa fields which quickly give way to the desert, and even the mud-brick homes on the fringes of Luxor have a village character, with chickens, ducks, donkeys

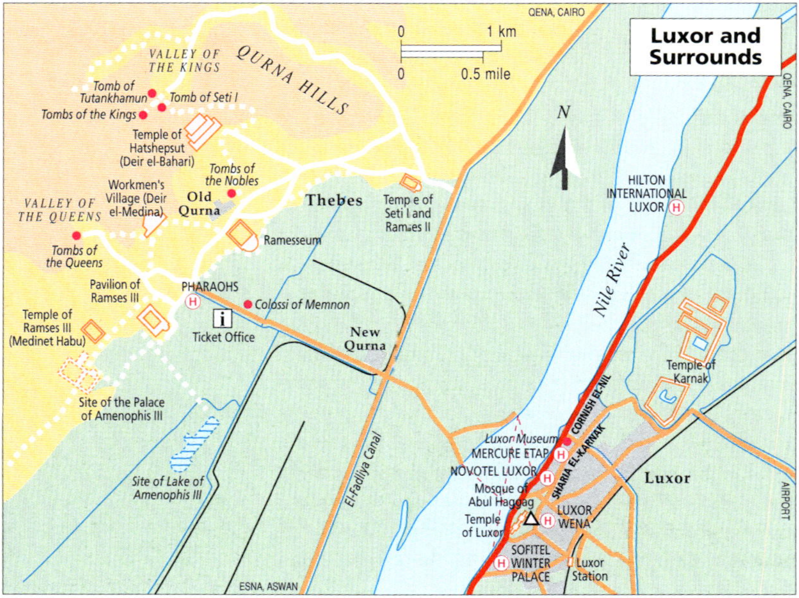

and goats roaming the streets and rooftops.

Luxor is a long, thin town which stretches for about 6km (3.5 miles) along the Nile but spreads only 2km (1 mile) inland at its widest. The magnificent **Temple of Luxor** is the focal point of the town centre, and the **Cornish el-Nil** (Sharia el-Bahr) esplanade runs the entire length of the waterfront. Just to the north of the Temple of Luxor, between the Cornish and Sharia el-Karnak, is a covered bazaar area full of shops selling a variety of antiques and souvenirs. From the Cornish, there are attractive views across the Nile to the green strip of cultivation on the west bank and its backdrop of arid red mountains.

Temple of Luxor ***

Luxor's most obvious landmark is this magnificent complex of columns, statues and sphinxes, which lay buried beneath the Egyptian village until archaeological excavations began in the 19th century. The temple is situated in the town centre, between Cornish el-Nil and Sharia el-Karnak. The entrance is on Cornish el-Nil. Two gigantic statues of **Ramses II** stand in front of the mighty pylons that mark the temple entrance. Within, there are more colossi of Ramses and his queen, **Nefertari**, and the **Court** and **Hall of Amenophis**, the 18th-Dynasty Pharaoh who built much of the temple. An avenue of small sphinxes leads north from the entrance and in antiquity was merely part of a processional way which connected the Temple of Luxor with the temples of **Karnak**, almost 5km (3 miles) to the north. Open 06:00–21:00 winter, 06:00–22:00 summer.

Early Tourists

By the mid-19th century, Egypt had become a popular extension of the well-off traveller's grand tour through the antiquities of Greece, Turkey and Palestine. Among them were politicians like the English Benjamin Disraeli; artists such as Holman Hunt, Frederick Goodall, and David Roberts, whose Egyptian drawings inspired the design of the legendary Crystal Palace, built in London for the Queen's Jubilee of 1854. By the turn of the century, tourism in Egypt was already big business, with grand hotels such as Shepheard's in Cairo, the Winter Palace in Luxor and the Cataract in Aswan, as well as luxury steamers plying the Nile.

Amun

Most Egyptian deities had several aspects or attributes. Originally a minor god worshipped by the Thebans, Amun came to be the most important in the ancient pantheon during the **Middle Kingdom**. The war-god **Montu** and the fertility god **Min**, who were originally deities in their own right, became different aspects of Amun, and during the **New Kingdom** he metamorphosed into the sun-god **Amun-Ra**. He was not only the King of the gods but also the divine father of the Pharaoh, who ruled as the representative of the gods on earth. He is pictured as a blue-skinned man, wearing a tall crown and carrying the whip and crook of power.

Mosque of Abul Haggag ★

Perched atop the inner court of the Temple of Luxor, this attractive mosque, painted and tiled in mellow ochre and faded blue geometric patterns, dates from the 13th century and commemorates a local sheikh. Entrance is gained from Sharia el-Karnak, behind the Temple of Luxor, and visits are by arrangement.

Luxor Museum ★★★

Cornish el-Nil, two blocks north of Temple of Luxor. Do not miss this excellent museum. Second only to the Egyptian Antiquities Museum in Cairo in the wealth of its collection, the clearer, less cluttered modern layout of Luxor Museum makes its treasures all the more fascinating. Top exhibits include pink granite and black basalt statues from many dynasties, some calmly smiling, others grim and judgmental in their power. Items from the **Tomb of Tutankhamun** (most of whose treasures are in the Egyptian Antiquities Museum in Cairo) include a gorgeous golden cow's head, so well preserved that it might have been made yesterday, as well as a bed and model ships designed to ferry the Pharaoh to the afterlife. Make time, too, to look at many smaller but no less fascinating exhibits from Pharaonic and Roman times, which include coins, glassware, jewellery and tiny figurines. Open 09:00–13:00, 16:00–21:00 winter, 09:00–13:00, 17:00–22:00 summer.

Temple of Karnak ★★★

The temple is 5km (3 miles) north of the town centre on Sharia el-Karnak, and is well signposted. If Luxor is the high point of many visits to Egypt, then Karnak is the most thrilling part of any visit to Luxor. Taking in the whole complex in even superficial detail

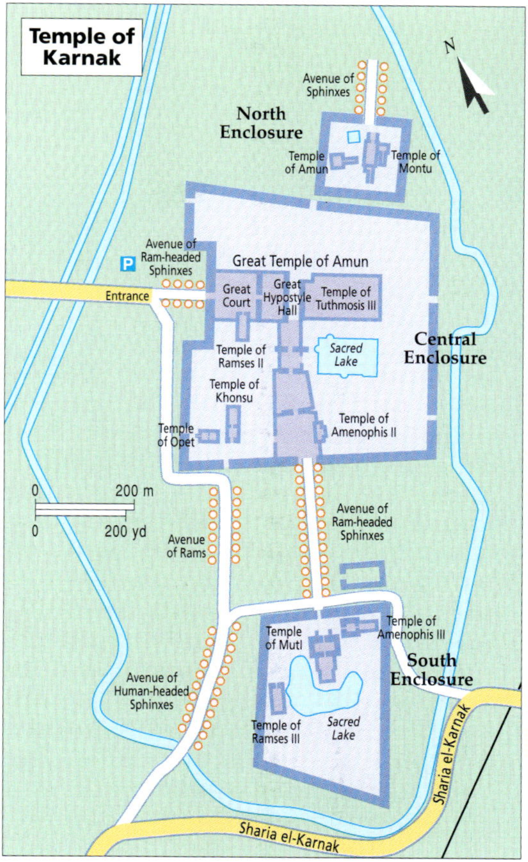

Columns

As the builders of the ancient Egyptian world learned to use stone as well as mud-brick, they began to use stone columns to support the roofs of their temples. These columns were sometimes carved to imitate the trunks of palm trees, papyrus reeds or lotus stems. During the time of the **Middle Kingdom**, columns may have been in the form of giant effigies of the ruling Pharaoh as **Osiris**, or they may have borne the face of the cow-goddess **Hathor** on their capitals. In the **Ptolemaic era**, the composite capital evolved, decorated with grapes, wheat bunches, vine leaves, lotus flowers and bunches of papyrus.

could take days; most people devote a half day or less to visiting the awesome **Temple of Amun**. Karnak is vast in its temporal as well as its physical dimensions. Begun in the Middle Kingdom, it was still being added to during the 25th Dynasty, 1300 years later. Dedicated to Amun, greatest of Egyptian gods, Karnak was more than just the spiritual centre of the kingdom. The temple and its priests came to control great estates and a huge work force, and eventually even to threaten the political power of the Pharaohs (see History, page 15).

Opposite: *The massive Temple of Karnak complex, the highlight of any visit to Luxor.*

Hieroglyphs

Hieroglyphic writing, with its complex set of symbols in the shape of animals, birds, people and geometric shapes, baffled Europeans until the early 19th century. In 1799 Napoleonic troops discovered a large inscription stone near **Rosetta**. It was inscribed not only with **hieroglyphs** but with their equivalent in **Ptolemaic Greek**. In 1801 the stone fell into the hands of the British, but it was a Frenchman, **Jean François Champollion**, who in 1823 finally cracked the code. The huge number of inscriptions on temples and tombs gives archaeologists a vast body of material to work with, and translation continues to this day. The Rosetta Stone remains in the British Museum.

Below: *A detail of the hieroglyphs on the Obelisk of Hatshepsut.*

It is worth visiting Karnak twice: once during the day, when you can see the scope and plan of the complex and look at its intricate and detailed inscriptions and murals, and a second time in the evening for the excellent **Sound and Light Show**. Entrance is by a processional avenue guarded by ranks of ram-headed sphinxes and leading to the **First Pylon**, a towering gateway, through huge, sloping walls that stand almost 45m (147ft) high, into the **Great Court**. On the south side a smaller pylon conducts you into the **Temple of Ramses III**, while on the east side two pink granite **colossi of Ramses II** guard the **Second Pylon**, opening into the **Great Hypostyle Hall**. Cluttered with vast pillars, this 6000 sq m (7176 sq yd) space is dim and shady even by day, and is genuinely ghostly after dark. Begun by **Amenophis III**, builder of the Temple of Luxor, it was completed by Ramses II. Two more pylon gateways lead you to the oldest section of the temple complex, with 14 pillars still standing. The most striking feature is the 29.2m (96ft) **Obelisk of Hatshepsut**.

Beyond this, the Fifth and Sixth Pylons lead into the **Central Court**, where the **Wall of Records** has inscriptions depicting the triumphs of the **Pharaoh Tuthmosis II**. Beyond this is the **Great Festival Temple of Tuthmosis III**.

East of this, beyond an expanse of more derelict foundations where restoration continues, is the **Sacred Lake**. To the southwest, the well-preserved **Eighth Pylon** is the most striking landmark above a field of toppled columns, walls and statuary, guarded by four of six original colossal statues. The best preserved is that of **Amenophis I**.

Sound and Light Show ★★★

Sound and Light shows take place at 18:15, 19:30, 20:45 and 22:00 in winter, one hour later in summer; there is at least one English language show each night, but check with your hotel or tour operator as there is a rotating schedule of languages. The show begins at the entrance to Karnak with a guided tour through the ghostly hypostyle halls, leading to tiers of seats overlooking the **Sacred Lake**, where lights pick out the pillars and statues as the show tells the millennia-long history of Thebes.

Above: *Palm trees and cane fields line the banks of a canal at Luxor.*

West Bank

The monuments of the West Bank are striking because they stand in grandiose isolation against a backdrop of lifeless, arid mountains, where the temple columns and colossi seem to grow out of the living rock of the Qurna Hills. The old-fashioned, brightly painted mud-brick houses of **Qurna village**, just west of the main road, provide splashes of colour against this barren landscape. Many villagers were relocated to the settlement of **New Qurna**, 4.5km (2.75 miles) closer to the river, on the **El-Fadliya Canal**, but some refused to move from their ancestral homes. Access to the West Bank is by ferry from the pier at the south end of the Cornish el-Nil, close to the **Novotel Hotel**, or via a new road bridge 9km (5.5 miles) south of Luxor which necessitates a long detour but is favoured by most escorted sightseeing tour companies. The sites of the West Bank cover an area of some 10 sq km (3.8 sq miles), beginning 3km (2 miles) from the ferry landing, and are connected by a purpose-built road.

Separate tickets are necessary for each site or group of sites (there are 18) and must be bought from the ticket office beyond the Colossi of Memnon. Tickets are not refundable, so unless you are on an escorted tour you need to plan your visit. Allow several days to take in the key sights at leisure. Opening times are 07:00–17:00 winter, 06:00–19:00 summer, unless otherwise stated.

Technical Terms

Technical terms used to describe details of tombs, temples and other ancient works crop up frequently. Some of these include:

- *Canopic jar:* stone or ceramic container for the organs removed during mummification.
- *Capital:* decorated top of a column.
- *Cartouche:* rounded rectangle surrounding the name of a god or Pharaoh, cut or painted on walls or pillars.
- *Hieroglyphs:* ancient Egyptian script using symbols and pictures to stand for consonants or complete words.
- *Hypostyle hall:* pillared hall.
- *Obelisk:* square-sided stone pillar with pyramidal top.

OZYMANDIAS

Inspired by reports and pictures drawn by travellers to Egypt, **Percy Bysshe Shelley** (1792–1822) wrote one of his best-known poems, an epitaph for a mythical despot: Ozymandias.

I met a traveller from an antique land
Who said: Two vast and trunkless legs of stone
Stand in the desert ... Near them, on the sand,
Half sunk, a shattered visage lies, whose frown,
And wrinkled lip, and sneer of cold command,
Tell that its sculptor well those passions read
Which yet survive, stamped on these lifeless things,
The hand that mocked them, and the heart that fed:
And on the pedestal these words appear:
'My name is Ozymandias, king of kings:
Look on my works, ye Mighty, and despair!'
Nothing beside remains. Round the decay
Of that colossal wreck, boundless and bare
The lone and level sands stretch far away.

Above: *The Colossi of Memnon mark the site of a vanished temple.*
Opposite: *The Temple of Hatshepsut on the west bank of the Nile near Luxor.*

Colossi of Memnon *

To the right of the main road, opposite the Memnon Hotel, 3km (2 miles) west of the ferry landing. Not enclosed. Two colossal seated statues mark the site, now covered by fields, of the vanished **Temple of Amenophis III**. Much damaged (they lack facial features), the colossi have been a tourist attraction for more than 2000 years, and in the time of the Ptolemies were believed by the Greeks to represent a mythical Ethiopian king, **Memnon**, who was killed by Achilles during the Trojan war.

Temple of Ramses III (Medinat Habu) **

Approximately 3.5km (2.25 miles) to the west of the ferry landing, to the south of the main road, clearly signposted. This huge, well-preserved temple was the last great project of the Pharaonic era. Three pillared **hypostyle halls** lead to an **inner sanctuary**. The most interesting facet of the building is the outer wall, which is densely engraved with **reliefs** depicting the defeat of the Sea Peoples (see History, page 17).

Ramesseum *

About 5km (3 miles) from the ferry landing, immediately to the east of the road, below Old Qurna village. Tumbled columns mark the site of this enormous **funerary temple**, now much ruined but worth visiting to see the **toppled colossus of Ramses II**, said to have inspired Shelley's Ozymandias.

Temple of Hatshepsut (Deir el-Bahari) ***

Situated about 6km (3.5 miles) from ferry landing, 750m (820yd) north of Old Qurna village. Queen Hatshepsut's funerary temple grows out of the towering pink cliffs into which it was built. **Hatshepsut**, daughter of the 18th-Dynasty ruler **Tuthmosis I**, was the first woman to rule Egypt in her own right. Superbly detailed reliefs within the colonnades of the temple recount her expansion of the empire's trade links with Punt (modern Somalia). Note the extremely realistic portrayals of the creatures of the Red Sea, which would do credit to any marine biologist today, and the king and queen of Punt, who are depicted as almost obese compared with the elegantly slender Egyptians. Column capitals depict the cow-goddess **Hathor** with Hatshepsut's own features. Other images of the Queen were defaced by her stepson and eventual successor, **Tuthmosis III**, who resented her power and desecrated her temples here and elsewhere, often replacing them with his own.

In later times, the temple became a Christian monastery, hence its alternative name, **Deir el-Bahari** (Northern Monastery). A crumbling mud-brick gateway to the south of the main road marks the site of the Roman-era settlement.

Early Archaeologists

The early European archaeologists were little better than the tomb robbers who preceded them, being far more interested in treasures and prestige than in knowledge. In the first half of the 19th century, tombs were looted of their contents, mummies were stripped of the jewellery buried with them, and statues dug up and carted off. In 1858, a new **Egyptian Antiquities Service** was created, headed by the French Egyptologist **Auguste Mariette**, and the government then began to control the excavations, while a new generation of investigative archaeologists took the place of the earlier treasure hunters.

Security Forces

Since the Luxor massacre, security has been tightened up at tourist areas all over Egypt and the security forces are much in evidence, with armed **uniformed police guards** at most large hotels and at all visitor attractions. Armed plain-clothes policemen accompany groups at all the ancient sites in Luxor, Aswan, Cairo and elsewhere, and these days the tourist coaches often travel in **guarded convoys**. Uniformed or plain-clothes police also ride shotgun on trains and buses, and there are several **security checkpoints**.

Above: *The shattered slopes of the Valley of the Queens hide their secrets well.*

Opposite: *This fresco in the tomb of Sennedjem, in the Deir el-Medina, depicts scenes from life in the ancient world.*

Valley of the Queens

About 4.5km (2.75 miles) from the ferry landing, 1.5km (0.75 mile) west of the Temple of Ramses III. More than 70 queens, princes and princesses were buried here. Their burial places were less lavish, but by no means less interesting, than those of the Pharaohs. They are less stylized in their decor, and the **tomb paintings** sometimes have a liveliness missing from those of the great Pharaonic tombs. Only a few tombs are open, of which two are well worth visiting.

Tomb of Nefertari ★★★

Only 150 people a day are admitted and only ten are allowed in at any one time; the easiest way to arrange tickets is through an agency. The tomb of Nefertari, favourite wife of **Ramses II**, is the finest in Egypt. None of her treasures survived the tomb robbers, but the three chambers are adorned from top to bottom with portraits of Nefertari making offerings to the gods and goddesses, including **Hathor** and **Osiris**. Open 08:30–12:00 and 13:00–16:00 winter, 07:30–12:00 and 13:00–17:00 summer.

Tomb of Amunherkhepshep ★★

This is the tomb of the son of **Ramses III**, and he died at the age of nine. The frescoes show the king handing his son over to the guardianship of **Anubis**, god of the dead. The mummified remains of a five-month-old foetus, discovered in the tomb, are displayed in a glass case within.

Tombs of the Nobles ★★★

These tombs are situated 5km (3 miles) from the ferry landing, immediately northwest of Old Qurna. Very few people visit the tombs, yet they are among the most fascinating relics of ancient Egypt. Some **400 tombs** are

Nefertari's Tomb

Discovered in 1904, Nefertari's tomb was closed in 1986 for the restoration of the **finest wall paintings** of any Egyptian tomb. The murals had been damaged by humidity and the formation of salt crystals and have been painstakingly restored at a cost of US$6 million by the **Department of Antiquities** and the **Getty Conservation Organization**. To control the damaging humidity, only 150 visitors a day are allowed in, and some experts say even that figure may be too high.

scattered around this area, spanning the period from the 6th Dynasty until the Roman era, and around a dozen are well worth a visit. They are divided into five groups, and you need a separate ticket for each group. All are **elaborately decorated**, and while the huge tombs of the Pharaohs are decorated with highly stylized frescoes recounting their achievements and conquests, the smaller tombs of their ministers and advisers are built on a more human scale and their colourful decorations tell of everyday life, with scenes of hunting, sailing and village life.

Workmen's Village (Deir el-Medina)

This site, just south of the main complex of the valley tombs, was the home of the craftsmen who built the tombs of the Valley of the Kings. Both the modern names are misleading: 'Deir el-Medina' means 'monastery of the town', a name stemming from the settlement of early Christian monks here. And the skilled artisans who lived here were far more than mere labourers, as their work shows. Their own tombs, marked by miniature 2m (6ft) pyramids of stone and mud brick, are decorated with motifs borrowed from those of their royal employers. The foundations of more than 70 houses can also be seen. Open 06:00–17:00 in summer, 06:00–16:00 in winter.

ANUBIS

Jackal-headed Anubis was the **god of death**, of embalming and mummification. According to the *Book of the Dead*, it was he who judged the Pharaoh after his death, weighing his heart against the feather of truth. His black skin is also symbolic of the fertile black silt of the **Nile**.

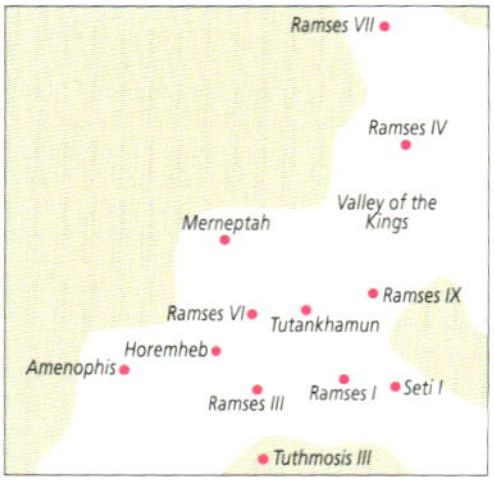

Valley of the Kings

This valley is located about 7km (4 miles) from the ferry landing, to the northwest of Old Qurna village. At first glance, there seems to be nothing to see in the Valley of the Kings – a narrow cleft between lifeless, sun-blasted hills of shattered rock. The tombs are tunnelled deep into the hillside, and successive Pharaohs took ever more labyrinthine precautions against their tombs and their treasures being discovered and looted. Despite all these precautions, only a single tomb – that of the boy-king **Tutankhamun** – has ever been found almost intact. The **Tomb of the Sons of Ramses II**, which was recently discovered by US archaeologist Kent Weeks and is still being excavated, has become the focus of much excitement. With about 130 chambers revealed so far, and more expected, it is the largest tomb in the Valley of the Kings and probably the largest in Egypt.

The tombs themselves are a bit of an anticlimax, for some of them are no more than tunnels in which a few scraps of painting or relief are the only indication of their antiquity. Over sixty tombs have been discovered. Not all of them are open at any one time, as excavations continue at several, and very few visitors in any case will wish to visit them all The most impressive include:

Tomb of Seti I ***

If you have time to visit only one tomb, this has to be the one not to miss. A deep corridor, divided by two intermediate chambers, leads approximately 100m (109yd) into the rock, and the **reliefs** which adorn its walls are in excellent condition. The ceiling of the tomb itself is decorated with sacred texts and sacred vultures (venerated by the ancient Egyptians because of their association with death). It has recently been extensively restored.

Tomb of Seti II **

Fine **murals** decorate the entrance to this tomb and a **mummy** (probably not that of Seti II) can be seen in the mortuary chamber.

Nut and Geb

Nut is the queen of the night and the mother of **Isis**, **Osiris**, **Seth** and the kite-goddess **Nephthys**. She was the wife (and sister) of the earth-god **Geb**, who is pictured as a reclining man. Geb divided Egypt between his sons, giving Upper Egypt to Seth and Lower Egypt to Osiris.

Below: *The entrance to one of the hundreds of tombs in the Valley of the Kings.*

Tomb of Ramses VI ***

Ramses VI took over the unfinished tomb of his predecessor, thus getting a head start in construction of his own burial place. The tomb reaches 83m (90yd) into the hillside and its walls are richly decorated with complex illustrations of the **Egyptian sacred texts**, the *Book of the Dead*, the *Book of the Caverns* and the *Book of Gates* – a kind of guide to the afterlife, recounting the steps of the dead king's passage into the beyond. The shattered stone **sarcophagus** in the tomb chamber is watched over by a painted ceiling portraying the sky-goddess **Nut**. This tomb has recently been restored.

Above: *In the tomb of Ramses VI, colourful paintings depict scenes from the* Book of the Dead.

Tomb of Ramses IX **

Nut is also a central feature in the ceiling-painting of this tomb, which also has an outer chamber that has been dramatically decorated with **paintings** of demigods and mythical beasts.

Tomb of Merneptah **

The entrance chamber of this tomb, with its reliefs of **Isis** and her sister-goddess **Nephthys**, is its finest feature. Within is a passageway adorned with illustrations and texts from the *Book of Gates* and leading 80m (87yd) down to the burial chamber.

Tomb of Tutankhamun *

Almost a compulsory stop on most organized tours of Egypt, and undoubtedly the best-known of all the many tombs, this is a real anticlimax. Its treasures, unearthed by the great Egyptologist **Howard Carter** in 1922, are all housed in the Egyptian Antiquities Museum and the tomb itself is little more than an empty chamber, dwarfed by comparison with the graves of the greater Pharaohs that surround it.

HOWARD CARTER

The excavation of **Tutankhamun's tomb** was the work of British archaeologist Howard Carter, who was convinced that the intact tomb was in the **Valley of the Kings** – a possibility discounted by many other Egyptologists. He was proved right in 1922, after six years of digging, when he found first a flight of steps, then the sealed door into the tomb. He later wrote: ' ... details of the room within emerged slowly from the mist, strange animals, statues and gold – everywhere the glint of gold ... I was struck dumb with amazement, and when Lord Carnarvon, unable to stand the suspense any longer, inquired anxiously, "Can you see anything?" it was all I could do to get out the words, "Yes, wonderful things."'

Luxor at a Glance

Best Times to Visit

In **winter** and **spring** (November to April), the days are warm and sunny, and the nights cool, or even chilly. The hot weather begins in May, and from June to September it can be unpleasantly hot day and night. Rain is rare at any time of year. With Egypt's tourism recovering rapidly from its severe decline, many of the main tourist sights and hotels are crowded, especially in winter.

Getting There

International scheduled flights by **EgyptAir** from London and some European cities. Charter flights from the UK and several European cities. Domestic flights from Cairo, Aswan and Alexandria.

Highway 2 connects Luxor with the northern towns of the Lower Nile and Cairo, and with Aswan. **Highway 44** connects Luxor with Hurghada via Qena and Safaga. Coaches run on all these routes. Tourist coaches may be required to travel in convoy with a police escort.**Trains** to Cairo and all points between Luxor and Aswan. Many **river cruisers** operate between Aswan and Luxor. ***Feluccas*** with crew can also be hired, but travelling down the river from Aswan is preferable to the slow journey upstream from Luxor.

Getting Around

Minibuses, **taxis** and open **horse-drawn carriages** are available in town. **Bicycles** can be hired at all the hotels and are ideal for visiting Karnak and the West Bank. Passenger **ferries** cross the river between the jetty just north of the Novotel (at the southern end of Cornish el-Nil) and the West Bank jetty. Visiting the West Bank sites as part of an organized tour group can be less hassle than doing it on your own, because this would involve queuing for tickets and finding your way around while evading the attentions of whispering 'guides' whose knowledge of the area and command of English are minimal, but who constantly demand baksheesh.

Where to Stay

Luxor has its fair share of luxury, mid-range and budget hotels, most of them along the river with fine views. Many of the best are along **Sharia Khaled Ibn el-Walid**, the southern extension of the **Cornish el-Nil**. There are a number of very cheap hotels on the **West Bank** but none can be recommended.

Luxury

Winter Palace Hotel, Cornish el-Nil, tel: (095) 380-422, fax: (095) 374-087. Grand hotel built in 1897. Pools, tennis court, dress code (no shorts or T-shirts).

Hilton International Luxor, Karnak, tel: (095) 374-933, fax: (095) 376-571. The only luxury hotel at Karnak, with gardens and pool, 500m (547yd) from the temple.

Mid-Range

Club Med Belladonna Resort, Sharia Khaled Ibn el-Walid, tel: (095) 384-000, fax: (095) 380-879. Full board, enclave of French bourgeois comfort on the Nile.

Mercure ETAP Hotel, Cornish el-Nil, tel: (095) 374-944, fax: (095) 374-912. Higher end of the four-star range with garden and Nile views.

Novotel Luxor, Sharia Khaled Ibn el-Walid, tel: (095) 380-925, fax: (095) 380-972.

Pharaohs Hotel, Medinet Habu, 100m (109yd) north of Temple of Ramses III, tel and fax: (095) 310-702. The only satisfactory place to stay on the West Bank.

Budget

Luxor Wena Hotel, Sharia el-Karnak, 100m (109yd) east of Luxor Temple, tel and fax: (095) 380-018. Good value three-star with relaxed garden restaurant/bar, very central.

Where to Eat

Luxor has disappointingly few places to eat outside the main hotels, which offer the usual international tourist menu.

East Bank

Winter Palace Hotel, see Where to Stay. Elegant

Luxor at a Glance

surroundings and service, dress code, food average.
Kaskade Restaurant, see Novotel Luxor Hotel. Pleasant café terrace in hotel gardens overlooking Nile.
Marhaba Restaurant, Tourist Bazaar, corner of Sharia el-Karnak and Cornish el-Nil, tel: (095) 372-633. Rooftop terrace. Food average, choice of Western and Egyptian, views of river and temple.
Tiba Star, moored at Cornish el-Nil opposite corner of Cornish and Sharia el-Karnak, tel: (095) 380-855, no fax. Floating restaurant and disco with belly dancers. Egyptian and international.
Sindbad Restaurant, see Luxor Wena Hotel. Cheerful if shabby garden bar and restaurant with good basic Western and Egyptian dishes. Value for money.
Ali Baba Café, corner of Sharia el-Karnak and Luxor Wena Hotel Gardens, no fax or telephone. Small rooftop café overlooking the Temple of Luxor. Downstairs you can sample apple tobacco in an Egyptian shisha (water pipe).
Café Bar Tutankhamun, north side of car park, Temple of Karnak, no tel or fax. Cold soft drinks, snacks.
Restaurant Café Horus, north side of car park, Temple of Karnak, no tel or fax. Cold drinks, light snacks, takeaways.

West Bank
Pharaohs Hotel Restaurant, see Where to Stay. Adequate restaurant, simple meals.

Shopping

Luxor is the best place outside **Cairo** for shopping. There are numerous shops in the Tourist Bazaar, Sharia el-Karnak; on sale are leather goods, sandals, Egyptian cotton T-shirts, pants and *galabiyehs* (the nightshirt-like robe worn by Egyptian men and women); copies of finds from the tombs; paintings on papyrus. One of the best places to buy the latter is **Dr Ragab's Papyrus Museum**, a floating shop in front of the Mercure ETAP Hotel, where you can buy more or less authentic copies of original frescoes as well as some more imaginative works. On the West Bank at **Qurna** are workshops selling alabaster cups and vases. Haggle for the best price – there is no such thing as a fixed price in Luxor.

Tours and Excursions

Misr Travel, Winter Palace Parade, Cornish el-Nil, tel: (095) 380-951, fax: (095) 380-950, organizes full- and half-day **guided tours** of the West Bank, Dendera and Abydos, felucca trips, floating hotel cruises to Aswan, and coach and train tickets.
Felucca touts will undoubtedly accost you along the Cornish el-Nil, and spending at least an hour on the river towards sunset is mandatory. Longer half-day or full-day **felucca trips** can also be made to Banana Island, a 'desert island' in the river 5km (3 miles) down the river.
Balloons Over Egypt, PO Box 52, Sharia Khaled Ibn el-Walid – desks in lobbies of Hilton, Sheraton and Isis hotels, tel: (095) 376-515, fax: (095) 370-638 – offers early morning **balloon flights**, starting on the West Bank and drifting over the valleys of the tombs and the Qurna Hills into the desert, where you are greeted by a champagne breakfast.
Budget hotels will arrange a **donkey** tour of the West Bank; this is the least comfortable way of seeing the area.

Useful Contacts

Tourist Office, Tourist Bazaar, corner of Cornish and Sharia el-Karnak, open 08:00–20:00. It is a fairly useless operation – **Misr Travel** is a better source of information.

LUXOR	J	F	M	A	M	J	J	A	S	O	N	D
AVERAGE TEMP. °F	75	82.5	84	91.5	104	106	107.5	106	102	93	85	75
AVERAGE TEMP. °C	24	28	29	33	40	41	42	41	39	34	29.5	24
HOURS OF SUN DAILY	11	11	11	11	12	12	12	12	12	11	11	11
RAINFALL	0	0	0	0	0	0	0	0	0	0	0	0

6
Aswan and the Upper Nile

South of Luxor, the corridor of cultivated land on either side of the Nile narrows, and towns become fewer and further between. The most striking of all the temples along the river between Luxor and Aswan are the work of the rulers of the **Ptolemaic Dynasty**, who in the three centuries of their rule extended their power as far as Nubia, building as they went. Their temples show not only **Hellenistic** influence but also a truly Greek sense for location, and each is magnificently sited.

Aswan, where dams were built by the British and, under Nasser, by Soviet engineers, was in ancient times the site of the first cataract (waterfall) on the Nile and thus marked, as it does today, the end of uninterrupted navigation on the river.

South of Aswan, the waters of the artificial **Lake Nasser** stretch almost 300km (180 miles) south into the Nubian desert, where the fantastic temples of Abu Simbel, rescued from the rising waters of the lake in a spectacular UNESCO operation during the 1960s, stand close to Egypt's southern border with Sudan. Aswan is virtually the last settlement of any size in southern Egypt: the small town of **Abu Simbel** exists purely to service visitors to the temples, and the wastes of the Nubian desert are virtually uninhabitable.

Just flying over this barren land of dunes and shattered rock is an awesome experience and a reminder of how much the life-giving waters of the Nile shaped ancient Egyptian civilization and continues to shape the lives of almost every Egyptian today.

Don't Miss

*** **High Dam:** amazing Soviet engineering.
*** **Temples of Philae:** attractive island temples rescued from the rising lake.
*** **Temples of Abu Simbel:** perhaps the most striking of all ancient sites, where 20m (66ft) colossi stand above the lake.
** **Temple of Horus:** at Edfu on the Nile, dwarfing modern buildings, stands this 3rd-century BC temple.
** **Kom Ombo:** temple to the crocodile god Sobek.

Opposite: *The Nile at Aswan, the river's highest navigable point.*

Above: *Colossal stone falcons at Edfu are sacred to Horus.*
Opposite: *The gigantic gateway of the Temple of Horus at Edfu.*

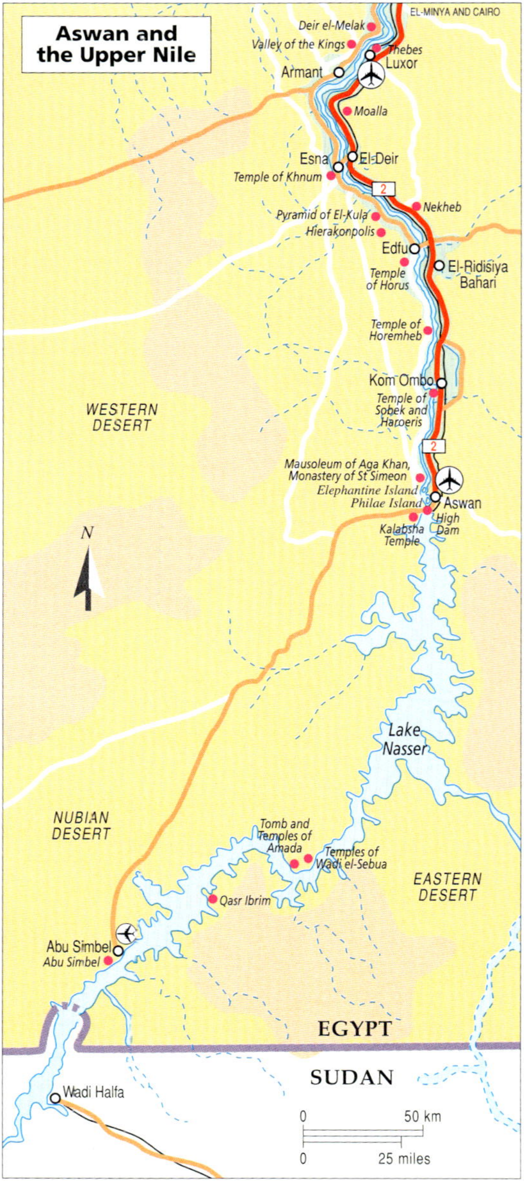

Aswan and the Upper Nile Climate

Aswan has a desert climate similar to Luxor's but with even longer, hotter summers. It is very pleasant in winter (though it can be cold at night), and unbearably hot in June–September. Rain hardly ever falls.

ESNA

Esna is a small commercial and market town located about 60km (38 miles) south of Luxor, situated on the west bank of the Nile.

Temple of Khnum **

The ticket office is 900m (980yd) from the crossroads at the town centre, quite close to the cruise ship dock. Only partially excavated, the most noteworthy feature of this temple to the ram-headed god **Khnum** (the god of the cataracts and of potters) is its hypostyle hall. Relatively recent in Egyptian terms, it was begun in the 2nd century BC by **Ptolemy VI**. It has a total of 24 columns supporting its stone-slabbed roof, which is still, remarkably, intact. Inscriptions show that it was still in use five centuries later, during the reign of the **Roman Emperor Decius**. Open 06:00–17:30 in winter, 06:00–18:30 in summer.

FELUCCAS

The tall, triangular gaff-rigged sail that propels the broad-beamed feluccas of the **Nile** is the same rig that carried Arab trade from the Straits of Gibraltar to the East Indies – and is still used on trading dhows in the **Arabian Gulf**, the **Red Sea** and the **Indian Ocean**. On the Nile, feluccas are nowadays used more by tourists than by traders, most cargoes being carried by motor barges, and a felucca cruise from Aswan down to Luxor can be one of the great Egyptian experiences. In the 19th century, it was normal practice for European tourists to ensure that their felucca was sunk for several days to kill off vermin living in its wooden hull.

EDFU

Approximately 115km (70 miles) south of Luxor on the west bank, Edfu's main attraction still manages to dwarf the modern buildings around it.

Temple of Horus **

Town centre. Begun in the reign of **Ptolemy III** in 237BC, this temple was completed only two centuries later, in the time of **Ptolemy XIII**, the father of **Cleopatra**. It was designed as a replica of an earlier temple, in a style that was already over a thousand years old when it was built, and is very well preserved. A gigantic, 36m (118ft) gateway is marked by two huge stone falcons, the sacred birds of **Horus**. Within the temple are, first, a 12-columned hypostyle hall covered with inscriptions showing the god in communion with the Pharaoh; a second hypostyle hall, giving way onto two antechambers; and finally the Sanctuary of Horus, the inner sanctum of the falcon-headed god. Open 07:00–16:00 in winter, 06:00–18:00 in summer.

Above: *Stone relief at the Temple of Sobek and Horus the Elder at Kom Ombo.*

Kom Ombo

Some 40km (25 miles) north of Aswan, Kom Ombo is the agricultural capital of a populous sugar-farming stretch of the Nile.

Temple of Sobek and Haroeris (Temple of Kom Ombo) ***

Approximately 4km (2.5 miles) south of the town centre, Kom Ombo benefits from its location. Standing on a jutting headland at a crook in the river, the fact that the temple has been ravaged by floods and by local builders who used it as a convenient source of building stone can be ignored. Crocodile-headed Sobek shared the temple with **Haroeris (Horus the Elder)** and the temple was begun in the 2nd century BC by **Ptolemy VI** and completed by later Ptolemaic and Roman rulers. In recognition of its dedication to the two gods, the temple is symmetrical along its long axis, with double entrances, courts, halls and sanctuaries to both Sobek and Haroeris. In the **Roman Sanctuary of Hathor**, to the south of the main temple, some of the mummified crocodiles discovered in a cemetery dedicated to the sacred animals are displayed. Open 08:00–16:00.

Horus and Seth

Horus, the falcon-headed son of **Osiris** and **Isis**, fought with his uncle **Seth**, god of evil, to avenge the murder of Osiris. The Pharaoh was regarded as the living incarnation of Horus, and the **'eye of Horus'**, which symbolized perfection and guarded against evil, was the forerunner of the blue amulets still found all over Greece, Turkey and the Middle East. Seth was the god not only of evil but of chaos, bringing storms and floods.

Aswan

Aswan, on the east bank of the Nile, has been the entrepôt of Upper Egypt since time immemorial. Here, the first of the mighty **Nile Cataracts** brought river shipping to a halt, and south of Aswan transport was by overland caravan. Here, the desert finally tightens its grip on the Nile, and the ribbon of greenery that has accompanied the traveller all the way upriver peters out once and for all. Ironically, the shores of the biggest body of fresh water in Egypt, the 500km (300 mile) **Lake Nasser**, are utterly barren and virtually uninhabited. Aswan's sights are low key (except for the brutally magnificent **High Dam**) but the small town itself is peaceful and pretty, with a palm-lined esplanade and greenery-covered islands dotting the Nile nearby. It is the obvious turnaround point for Nile cruisers, and the equally obvious resting place for travellers en route to the temples and statues of **Abu Simbel** that are closer to the southern end of Lake Nasser.

The most interesting sights to see in Aswan are on **Elephantine Island**, the long, palm-covered isle which is just offshore. Even were there nothing to see there, the felucca trip across to the island would still be well worth making, but in addition Elephantine is the site of **Yebu**, the main Egyptian trading centre and provincial capital in ancient times. Yebu was the ancient Egyptian for elephant, and elephants and their ivory formed a major part of its trade.

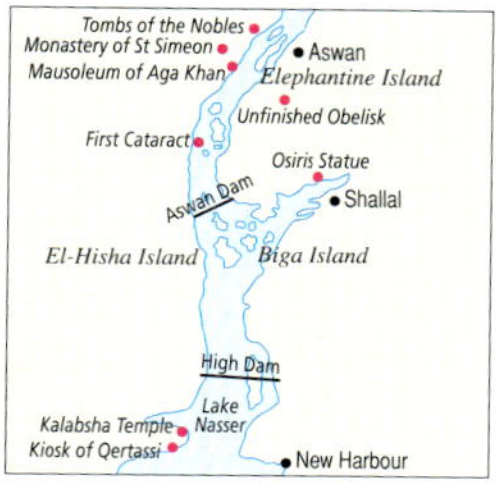

New Gateway

A new **international airport** opened at Aswan in July 1998, potentially making the southern city a new gateway for visitors arriving directly into Upper Egypt. With a capacity for 2500 passengers, the airport will eventually have a major impact on tourism to the region.

Yebu ruins and Nilometer **

At the southern end of Elephantine Island. The foundations of temples, including a temple to **Khnum**, the ram-headed patron deity of Aswan, are all that remains of Yebu. Cut into the cliff on the east side of Elephantine Island, the gradations of the Nilometer measured the flooding of the Nile. This in turn was a guide to the expected size of the crop down river, and was used to calculate how much taxation the farmers could bear each year. The Nilometer is inscribed in **Greek**, **Latin** and **Arabic** as well as in **hieroglyphs**, indicating that successive generations of rulers found it useful. Open 08:30–18:00.

Nubia Museum ***

South end of town, near Basma Hotel. Housed in a modern building amid gardens, this is the best museum in Egypt, tracing the history, arts and crafts of Nubia from prehistoric times to the present day. There is an artificial cave with prehistoric rock carvings, a Fatimid tomb and a model Nubian house. Open 09:00–13:00 and 17:00–20:00.

Below: *Whitewashed walls and domes are typical of Nubian village architecture.*

GRAFFITI

All over Egypt, cut painstakingly into the soft limestone of age-old columns or tomb walls and defacing the original inscriptions, you will see later graffitti, in **Greek**, **Latin** or **modern** characters; the names of soldiers of Napoleon's army, or of later visitors. During the 19th century, it was normal for well-off European and American tourists to climb the **Great Pyramid** and carve their names into its summit. At **Philae**, two English adventurers on their way home from Abyssinia, 'having spent 16 years in that country in the service of H. Salt Esq.' (Salt was then British consul in Cairo), left a lengthy testimonial in the stones of Trajan's palace.

Island of Plants (Kitchener's Island) ★

Approximately 500m (547yd) west of Elephantine Island lies this luxuriously planted island whose gardens were created by **General Kitchener**, the British consul general in Egypt, in 1910–11.

Attractions on the west bank of the Nile include the **Mausoleum of the Aga Khan**, the dome of which is visible from the river, and the 6th-century desert **Monastery of St Simeon**. Open 09:00–17:00, the monastery, now ruined, once provided accommodation for 300 monks.

High Dam and Lake Nasser ★★

Some 17km (10.5 miles) south of Aswan. As if to belittle the achievements of the Pharaohs by underlining those of a planned political economy, **Soviet engineers** lent their skills to Nasser's government to pen up the Nile once and for all behind concrete. The statistics are quite numbing: 3600m (3937yd) long and 111m (364ft) high at its highest point, the dam contains enough concrete and stone to build the Great Pyramid 20 times over. Damming the waters of the Nile created an **inland sea** almost 500km (300 miles) long which crosses the border between Egypt and Sudan. More than 40 towns and villages, and the homes of some 40,000 people, vanished beneath the rising waters, most of the **Nubian villagers** being resettled in and around Aswan. The High Dam has a certain magnificence, but the view is less than startling and unless you are a big fan of feats of engineering it must take a low place on your agenda. Open 09:00–17:00

Kalabsha Temple ★★

Next to the High Dam. Like Philae and Abu Simbel, this temple was rescued from the rising waters of **Lake Nasser** and moved to a new location. Massive and largely unadorned, the fort-like temple was built by **Augustus** and dedicated to the Nubian fertility god **Mandulis**. Open 09:00–17:00.

Philae (Agilika Island)

The island on which the temples of Philae originally stood was partially flooded by the construction of the **first Aswan Dam** in 1902 and completely submerged by the building of the **High Dam**. Between 1972 and 1980 the ruins were dismantled and rebuilt on Agilika, 2km (1 mile) south of the Aswan Dam, well above the water line. The most striking buildings are the **Palace (Kiosk) of Trajan**, the **Temple of Hathor** and the **Temple of Isis**, which are surrounded by the less impressive foundations of older temples. The earliest buildings date from the 4th century BC, the later ones from the **Ptolemaic and Roman era**. Open 07:00–16:00 winter, 10:00–17:00 summer.

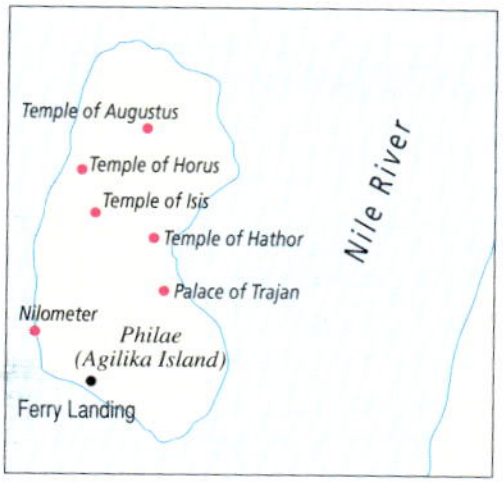

Bes and Taweret

Fat and gnome-like **Bes** was the god of music and dancing and also one of the protectors of both pregnant women and newborn babies, whom he guarded against the demons. **Taweret**, with the head of a hippo, the legs of a lioness and the tail of a crocodile, also protected women in childbirth.

Palace of Trajan ***

With its 14 towering columns, this is the most striking of the ruins of Philae. Built for the Roman emperor **Trajan**, it was never completed, because he died and the project was abandoned. Its friezes show Trajan offering wine and incense to **Isis**, **Osiris** and **Horus**.

Temple of Hathor ***

Built by the **Ptolemies** but embellished by the **Romans** in the time of **Caesar Augustus**, the Temple of Hathor is adorned with carvings of music and celebration dedicated to **Hathor** and to **Bes**, the god of music and pleasure.

Temple of Isis ***

The largest building on the island, this temple is entered by a gateway between two great pylons showing scenes of the Ptolemaic Pharaohs triumphing in battle. **Ptolemaic** and **Roman** scenes are in some places defaced by crosses carved by early **Christians**, who used the temple as a church, as are some of the carvings of Isis suckling the infant **Horus**.

Opposite: *Mausoleum of the Aga Khan on the west bank of the Nile at Aswan.*
Below: *The Temple of Isis and the Palace of Trajan at Philae were rescued from the rising flood waters of the Nile.*

Daughters of Ra

Sekhmet, the lion-headed daughter of **Ra**, was sent by him to chastise impious mankind. **Bastet**, the cat-goddess, another of Ra's daughters, could also be an instrument of Ra's vengeance but was more generally regarded as one of the deities of happiness. Their sister, cow-headed **Hathor**, was a benevolent goddess, associated with love and joy and a protector of women. Between her horns she bears the sun disc.

Abu Simbel

The architectural feats of the ancient Egyptians seem to inspire modern engineers to outdo them, and the rescue of temples and statues built by **Ramses II** at Abu Simbel from the rising Nile are no exception. The temples had to be cut free of the cliff face out of which they were carved. Then, at a cost of over US$40 million, they were transported to a site 65m (213ft) above the waterline and rebuilt against an artificial cliff. The project was completed in 1968. Abu Simbel lies 300km (180 miles) south of Aswan, on the bank of **Lake Nasser**. Open 06:00–17:00. The spectacular new computer generated Sound and Light Show plays on the face of the Great Temple.

Great Temple of Ramses II (Temple of Ra-Harakhty) ***

Located 1.5km (0.75 mile) from Abu Simbel. The four gigantic, seated figures of **Ramses II** that guard the entrance to the temple are among the most evocative sights Egypt has to offer. Each is set on a carved pedestal 4m (13ft) high and the statues themselves are 20m (65ft) high. A statue of the hawk-headed sun god **Ra** stands above the entrance. Inside, the walls are covered with carvings of Ramses II triumphing over the **Hittites** at the battle of **Kadesh**, while in the sanctuary are statues representing **Ra-Harakhty** (one of the aspects of Horus), **Ramses II**, **Amun** and **Ptah**. Open 07:00–16:00 winter, 07:00–17:00 summer.

Below: *The colossal statues at Abu Simbel were relocated to save them from the rising waters of Lake Nasser.*

Temple of Hathor ***

Next to Temple of Ramses II. Though dwarfed by its neighbour, this temple is nonetheless striking. It is guarded by six 10m (33ft) statues of **Ramses**, his queen, **Nefertari**, and their sons and daughters. Heads of the goddess **Hathor** adorn each of the six pillars of the hypostyle hall, and murals in the chambers leading off it depict the goddess. Open 07:00–16:00.

Aswan at a Glance

Best Times To Visit

From **November–March** the days are hot and sunny but nights can be a bit chilly. Summer (April–October) is stiflingly hot both during the day and night.

Getting There

Flights to Aswan from Abu Simbel, Cairo, Luxor and Hurghada. Flights to Abu Simbel from Aswan and Cairo. Main **highway** from Luxor to Aswan. Regular **express coaches** connect all points with Luxor and the north. **Trains** between Luxor and Aswan stop at Edfu, Esna and Kom Ombo. **River cruisers** and **feluccas** ply between Aswan and Luxor.

Getting Around

Minibuses, **taxis** in all towns, plus **horse-drawn *caleches*** in Aswan. **Feluccas** sail to the Nile islands from Aswan waterfront and to Philae from above the High Dam.

Where to Stay

There is no classified, recommendable accommodation in Esna, Edfu or Kom Ombo. Visit from Aswan.

Aswan

Luxury

Aswan Oberoi Hotel, Elephantine Island, PO Box 62, Aswan, tel: (097) 314-667, fax: (097) 313-538. Superbly located five-star hotel with spectacular views.

Sofitel Cataract Hotel and **New Cataract Hotel**, Sharia Abtal el-Tahrir, tel: (097) 316-000, fax: (097) 316-011. Grand old hotel managed by five-star French group. New Cataract is a modern annex. Spectacular views and pool.

Abu Simbel

Only two classified hotels. No recommended budget options.

Luxury

Nefertari Abu Simbel, Abu Simbel, tel: (097) 400-509, fax: (097) 400-510. The only four-star hotel in Abu Simbel.

Mid-Range

Nobaleh Ramsis Hotel, Abu Simbel Tourist City, tel: (097) 400-380, fax: (097) 400-381. Small, comfortable, new hotel.

Where to Eat

Aswan is the only town with a wider choice of eating places, as there are only café-restaurants elsewhere to choose from.

Aswan

Old Cataract Hotel, see Where to Stay. Grand surroundings, average food.

Aswan Oberoi Hotel, see Where to Stay. Fantastic views, average food.

Aswan Moon Restaurant, Cornish el-Nil, no telephone or fax. Floating restaurant.

A score of mostly nameless small café-restaurants cluster along **Sharia el-Souq**, parallel to the waterfront – a good bet for those on a tight budget. None has a telephone or fax.

Abu Simbel

Hotel restaurants are the only option, see Where to Stay.

Tours and Excursions

Karnak Tourist Services, EgyptAir office, Aswan, tel: (097) 315-006, fax: (097) 315-005. Cruises, excursions, city tours, rail and coach tickets.

Aswan Cultural Centre, Cornish el-Nil. Nightly shows by Nubian dancers and musicians, including exciting mock stick-fight dances. Tickets from all hotels and tour agencies.

Sound and Light Show, Philae. Nightly show with rotating language schedule, tickets from all hotels and tour agencies.

Useful Contacts

Aswan

Tourist Information Office, Railway Station, tel and fax: (097) 312-811. Transport timetables, maps, brochures.

ASWAN	J	F	M	A	M	J	J	A	S	O	N	D
AVERAGE TEMP. °F	75	79	86	95	104	107.5	107.5	107.5	104	98.5	88	79
AVERAGE TEMP. °C	24	26	30	35	40	42	42	42	40	37	31	26
HOURS OF SUN DAILY	11	11	11	11	12	12	12	12	12	11	11	11
RAINFALL	0	0	0	0	0	0	0	0	0	0	0	0

7
Sinai and the Red Sea

Appropriately enough for a region where the first tourists (apart from pilgrims to St Catherine's Monastery on Mt Sinai) were hippies and beach bums, the highway to Sinai from Suez is Egypt's Route 66. Sinai's attractions are largely natural – magnificent sunshine, fine beaches, dazzling diving and stunning scenery. The Sinai peninsula is a wedge of desert between the **Gulf of Suez** in the west and the **Gulf of Aqaba** in the southeast, with the Egypt-Israel border running in an almost straight line from **Taba**, at the head of the Gulf of Aqaba, to **Rafah** on the Mediterranean coast.

Sinai's Mediterranean coastline is barren and sparsely inhabited, with few attractions for visitors between Rafah and the **Suez Canal**. To the west, the desert is bisected by the Suez Canal, one of the most awesome engineering works of the 19th century. The coast of the Gulf of Suez, where there is considerable offshore oil activity, is dotted with unattractive industrial development. Beyond the canal the **Eastern Desert** stretches down towards the south, past ancient monasteries to **Hurghada** and a growing number of coastal resorts.

The north shore of the Gulf of Aqaba boasts a combination of sandy beaches, year-round sunshine and superb coral reefs attracting sun-worshippers and scuba divers. Inland, there is savage and spectacular desert and canyon scenery, and Egypt's highest mountain, with a 1500-year-old monastery perched on its slopes. Sinai was the scene of fierce fighting during both the 1967 **Arab-Israeli War**, when it was seized and fortified

Don't Miss

*** **Monastery of St Catherine:** on the slopes of Mt Sinai stands this 6th-century Orthodox monastery.
*** **Mt Sinai:** superb desert panorama from the accessible top of Egypt's second-tallest peak.
** **Coloured Canyon:** colourful natural rock strata amid desert surroundings.
** **Pharaoh's Island:** it is an enjoyable day trip to this Gulf island with its Crusader fortress and beach.

Opposite: *Fire coral and shimmering shoals of fish in the Red Sea.*

SINAI AND RED SEA CLIMATE

Sinai is pleasantly sunny and warm in winter (cool at night), very hot in summer. Best visited in **winter**, **spring** and **autumn** but can be visited year-round, especially for beach and diving holidays.

Opposite: *Heading out by boat to the superb dive sites off Hurghada.*

by Israel, and in the 1973 War, when the Egyptians attempted to reconquer the region only to be beaten back once again to the west bank of the Canal. It was returned to Egypt in 1982. Sinai's native **Bedouin** population are now far outnumbered by settlers from western Egypt, attracted not only by the offer of lucrative jobs in tourism but also by a government resettlement plan which includes construction of a vast tunnel to bring Nile water to irrigate the Sinai Peninsula.

Hurghada

About 525km (320 miles) south of Suez and 220km (136 miles) northeast of Luxor on the west shore of the Red Sea, Hurghada has evolved rapidly from a small port and divers' resort into a vast, unattractive sprawl of resort hotels that stretches some 20–30km (12–19 miles) either side of the original harbour. The name Hurghada has now come to cover the original harbour settlement, properly called **Ghardaqa** (now a city of some 300,000), as well as the earliest resort area, **Sigala**, some 5km (3 miles) to the south, and the New Hurghada hotel strip which extends for kilometres southward.

The scenery around Hurghada is uninspiring, a seemingly endless desert coastal plain giving way to a range of low arid hills some 10–20km (6–12 miles) inland, and the

Sinai and the Red Sea

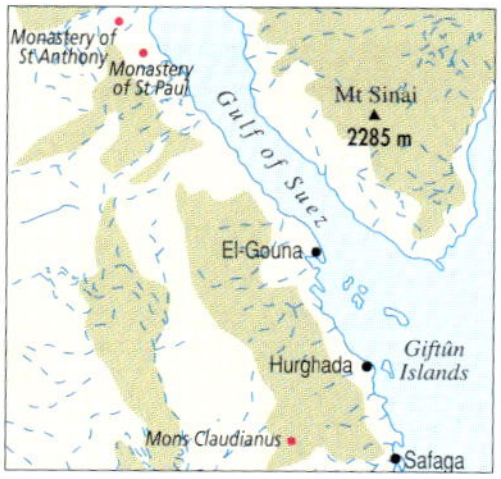

beaches are not sandy but rather a dusty reddish grit. Hurghada's redeeming features include reliable winter sunshine, which attracts holiday-makers from all over northern Europe, including large numbers of Russians (though not really in large enough numbers to fill the 30,000 hotel rooms the area already has, let alone the 60,000 which were already under construction when this book was researched).

The area's real attractions are underwater, with some spectacular diving close inshore around the **Giftun Islands**, as well as further up and down the coast. There is a good chance of seeing white-tipped sharks, eagle rays, and giant morays, as well as huge numbers of smaller sea creatures.

Hurghada's Reefs

Hurghada's reefs have been damaged by too many dive boats anchoring on them, and with more than 700 boats operating in local waters the potential for damage is huge. The **Hurghada Environmental Protection Conservation Association**, HEPCA, was formed in 1992 and operates a training programme for local boat captains as well as a network of low-impact mooring buoys at the busiest dive sites. The reefs are patrolled by national park rangers from the **Egyptian Environmental Affairs Authority** and rules against anchoring on the reef are more strictly enforced than in the past.

Safaga *

About 60km (38 miles) south of Hurghada, attempts are being made to turn this shabby port and freight rail terminus into a secondary resort area, with self-contained **hotel complexes** being built on the coast north of town. With the slump in tourism, much of the development in the area has stalled and it is hard to see why anyone would want to come here except to dive the offshore reefs – less crowded and in better shape than Hurghada's. Another 85km (55 miles) further to the south is the port of **Quseir**, still off the beaten track for most visitors.

El-Gouna **

Just 22km (14 miles) north of Hurghada Airport and 16km (10 miles) north of Hurghada Harbour stands the newest, most luxurious **tourism resort** in Egypt. In stark contrast to the unplanned sprawl of Hurghada, El-Gouna is the first resort in Egypt to be systematically planned. Opened in 1997, it covers 7 million square metres of formerly desert seashore, landscaped into **tropical gardens**, **lagoons** and **golf courses**. El-Gouna

Egypt's Tourism Net

You can hunt for your hotel accommodation throughout Egypt on the Egypt's Tourism Net website, which is found at (http://www.tourism.egnet.net). It lists hotels from one-star and below to five-star and above, countrywide. You can search by category, location, name and/or the existence of an e-mail address.

has its own hospital (with hyperbaric chamber for diving accidents), a US PGA-standard 18-hole golf course (the best in Egypt), watersports school, nursery, casino, shopping arcades, open-air amphitheatre and no fewer than three dive centres. It even has its own airport.

The resort consists of six luxury hotels, as well as condominium apartments and private villas. It is pitched at the wealthy of the Middle East (one hotel has 25 rooms set aside for royalty), but if you are prepared to rough it in a mere three-star you can also revel in the restaurants and other facilities of its luxury neighbours.

Deir Anba Antunius (Monastery of St Anthony) **

Some 40km (25 miles) west of Zafrana on the Hurghada-Suez coastal highway. Founded as early as the 4th century but looted by desert raiders in the 15th, the Monastery of St Anthony rivals that of St Catherine's on Mt Sinai in terms of location if not in the wealth of its interior, and outdoes it in terms of glorious isolation. The monastery sits beneath the beetling crags of the **Eastern Desert** where it begins to rise to its plateau. Within the high, 10th-century walls are a 12th-century **church**, its interior covered with well-preserved **frescoes**, and a later medieval keep. The cave in which St Anthony (the Christian church's first hermit) had his retreat is 2km (1 mile) above at the end of a steep cliff path. To the southeast lies the smaller, and architecturally less important, **Monastery of St Paul**. Paul fled to the Eastern Desert from Alexandria during the persecutions of the 3rd century. The monastery was built by his followers after his death around the cave in which he lived. Open 08:00–16:00.

Below: *St Anthony's Monastery sits beneath the crags of the Eastern Desert.*

Left: *Ocean-going freighters wait their turn to pass through the Suez Canal.*

The Suez Canal

The city of Suez is built on a long bay at the head of the eponymous Gulf, with its harbour area, **Port Tawfiq**, occupying a long promontory south of the city centre.

Suez was virtually levelled in the fighting between Egyptian and Israeli forces during both the 1967 and the 1973 wars, and reconstruction since then has done it very few favours. It is a drab industrial and commercial centre ringed by refineries and chemical works and – aside from the briefly interesting view it affords of the giant cruise ships, tankers and container vessels on the Canal – its only real interest for the visitor is its status as a transport hub between Lower Egypt and Sinai. Most travellers, however, prefer to travel directly between Cairo and places in Sinai such as Sharm el-Sheikh without stopping in Suez.

Suez Canal ***

At 167km long (105 miles) and almost 1km (1000yd) wide, the Suez Canal (really a series of man-made channels connecting a chain of salt lakes, the **Bitter Lakes**, which lies along the Isthmus of Suez) is a quite outstanding piece of 19th-century civil engineering and a tribute not only to the determination and skill of its French designer, **Ferdinand de Lesseps**, but also a tribute to the hundreds of anonymous Egyptian labourers who died during its construction. Closed for the eight years between 1967 and 1975, it now handles approximately 50 ships a day (only 60 per cent of its capacity) and earns Egypt some US$2 billion a year in tolls.

Hosni Mubarak

Mohammed Hosni Mubarak (1928–) entered the Egyptian Military Academy in 1947, becoming an officer in the air force in 1950 and rising swiftly to become its commander in chief in 1969, at the early age of 41. In 1973, his efficiency saved Egypt from complete humiliation in the October War, and in 1975 he was rewarded by President Sadat with the vice-presidency. He became president in 1981 after Sadat's assassination. Since then, he has given Egypt a veneer of free-market democracy (while cracking down ruthlessly on the militant Islamic opposition) and, unlike his predecessors, has allowed multi-party elections. These, however, have shown little sign of eroding his hold on power.

Above: *The elegant Suez Canal Authority Building in Port Said.*

Ismailia ★

There is a faint colonial feel to parts of Ismailia, which is not surprising as the modern town of 300,000 people was built during the Co-Dominium in the 1860s as the headquarters of the British canal administration and occupying force. It was named for the **Khedive Ismail**, the nominal head of state but a puppet of the colonial power in all but name. Ismailia stands on **Lake Timsah**, the smallest of the Bitter Lakes.

The house in the main street where Ferdinand de Lesseps lived while he oversaw the construction of his canal is now the **De Lesseps Museum**, housing documents, plans and photographs relating to the Canal. Open 09:00–16:00 daily, closed Tuesday. The **Ismailia Museum** on Mohammed Ali Quay has a collection of Graeco-Roman artefacts, including an interesting 4th-century AD mosaic depicting Dionysus and Phaedra. Open 09:00–16:00 daily.

Port Said ★

Port Said today shows little sign of living up to the reputation it had in its heyday as one of the world's wickedest ports (a reputation built on catering to the less salubrious urges of British troops and the world's merchant seamen). Built on an island at the northern end of the Canal in the mid-19th century, it fell into the doldrums after Egypt's defeat in the 1967 war with Israel (during which it was heavily bombed) and the closure of the Canal. With the Camp David agreement and the reopening of the Canal, it has been reconstructed, but is still far from being the Mediterranean's most exciting port of call. The **beaches** are pleasant enough, and it is a popular resort for Egyptians. The Canal today carries far less shipping than in its heyday, and Port Said's sole gesture in the direction of wickedness is its **duty-free shopping**, which attracts a clientele from all over the Middle East.

EGYPTIAN DRESS

While many Egyptians, especially men who live in larger towns, have adopted western dress, most rural people – and more traditionally-minded urban dwellers – still wear traditional costume. For men, this means the **galabiyeh**, a nightshirt-like robe that reaches to the ankles and may be coloured blue, grey, brown or for special occasions white. Many men also wear a turban-like headcloth or a small skullcap, also white. Women wear a similar garment, often black, with a coloured headscarf.

Sharm el-Sheikh

Close to the southern tip of the Sinai Peninsula, Sharm el-Sheikh is a natural harbour. It began to develop into a tourism destination under the Israeli occupation, then attracted the attention of scuba divers for whom it became a favourite base, and is now a fully fledged package holiday resort. There are some fears that over-development along the coast will damage the **coral reefs** and the once-pristine coastline, and the outskirts of the resort are one big construction site.

There is a secondary resort area at **Na'ama Bay**, 6km (3.5 miles) to the east of Sharm el-Sheikh, and it seems inevitable that the two will merge into one continuous resort strip in the near future.

There Goes the Neighbourhood

Egypt's largest integrated resort development will be built at Nabq, close to the **Nabq National Park**. Scheduled for completion in 2008, the resort will comprise 28 hotels on 28 sq km (11 sq miles) of desert and coastline. The resort's planners claim it will be environmentally sound, and the project has received approval from the EEAA, Egypt's environmental agency. A marina and dive school will be located away from Nabq's 8.5km (5 miles) of protected reef, and recreational salt-water lagoons will be created inland.

Ras Mohammed National Park ***

The waters around Ras Mohammed, the southern point of Sinai, offer some of the finest **diving** in the world, with 20 dive sites, superb coral and rich marine life including rays, sharks, morays and lionfish. Also in the deeper waters off Ras Mohammed are **wrecks**, including the *Dunraven*, which sank in 1876, the *Thistlegorm*, sunk by bombing during World War II, and also the *Carnatic*, which went down in 1879.

Left: *An aerial view of Ras Mohammed, the finest marine conservation area of the Red Sea.*

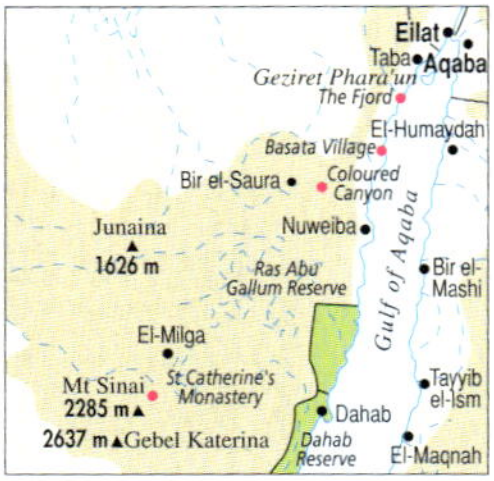

The Vital Phrases

- *Inshallah:* God willing (used in sentences such as: the bus will leave at one o'clock, inshallah)
- *Maalesh:* never mind
- *Bukra:* tomorrow (or the day after)
- *Shwayya:* slow down (or take it easy)
- *min fadlak* (m), *min fadlik* (f): please
- *shokran:* thank you
- *lah, shokran:* no, thank you
- *aywa:* yes
- *lah:* no

Dahab

About 85km (55 miles) north of Sharm el-Sheikh, Dahab, originally a Bedouin village on the coast, has become a backpackers' and divers' haven that sprawls along a sandy bay. A new town centre known as **Dahab City**, on the main road, has the bus station, bank and other official buildings among drab concrete apartment blocks. **Assala**, the original settlement, is 1.5km (0.75 mile) to the north, on Dahab Bay, and much more attractive. Snorkelling and diving are the main attractions.

St Catherine's Monastery ***

Situated 100km (62 miles) west of Dahab, 3km (2 miles) above the village of El-Milga. The monastery was built in AD527 in the reign of the **Byzantine Emperor Justinian I** on the site where the Bible claims God revealed himself to **Moses** as a **burning bush**. The fortress-like monastery is dedicated to St Catherine, and is maintained by a community of Greek Orthodox monks.

St Catherine's dates from an era when the Eastern Roman Empire was making a final effort to reassert its control over areas of the Middle East, and is a typical product of this final flowering of Byzantium. Within the massive walls (built in later, less stable times), the main landmarks of the monastery are the **Basilica**, endowed by the Emperor Justinian at the time of the monastery's founding in AD527, the **library**, containing thousands of **religious texts** in Greek, Hebrew, Latin and Arabic, an elegant new **museum**, dedicated to the history of the monastery and showing off some of its greatest treasures and most important icons, and a **mosque** dating from the early Fatimid era, built to ensure the continued tolerance of this Christian enclave by Muslim Arab rulers. Above the eastern

Below: *Taking it easy at Dahab on the coast of the Gulf of Aqaba.*

gate, the makeshift-looking lifting tackle and basket are the remains of a primitive **'elevator'** used instead of opening the gate. Open 09:00–12:00, closed Friday, Sunday and public holidays.

Above: *St Catherine's Monastery on the slopes of Mount Sinai.*

Mt Sinai ***

At 2285m (7497ft) Mt Sinai, above the monastery, is Egypt's second-highest mountain and is said to be where God delivered his **Ten Commandments** to **Moses**. The summit is reached by the **3000 Steps of Repentance**, cut by monks from St Catherine's as a penitential trail, or alternatively by the **'camel trail'** where you will undoubtedly be pestered by Bedouin camel drivers offering to take you to the summit for a price. The climb takes two to three hours and there are great views. Set off early to avoid the heat.

Jebel Katerina ***

Egypt's **highest peak**, 2637m (8651ft) high and 6km (3.5 miles) west of Mt Sinai, should be attempted only if you are a fit and experienced walker and climber. Be sure to take plenty of water with you.

Coloured Canyon **

Approximately 40km (25 miles) northwest of **Nuweiba**, along an unsurfaced road that should only be attempted by four-wheel-drive vehicles, the rock strata of this narrow gorge glow with colour.

Women in Egypt

Egypt is still very much a man's country. Sons are preferred to daughters, illiteracy is much higher amongst women than amongst men, and **clitoridectomy** (euphemistically referred to as 'female circumcision') is still widely practised, especially in rural communities. Forced to tread carefully where traditional **Islamic** sensibilities are concerned, government efforts to tackle these issues have been circumspect to say the least.

Package Tours

Even if you are a free spirit, travelling on a package holiday can be the best and one of the most affordable ways of getting to Egypt, doing what you want to do and seeing what you want to see. Package holidays are available from tour operators worldwide, but the best choice and the cheapest prices are in the UK, where there are tour companies specializing in everything from **beach holidays** in Hurghada to **camel safaris** in Sinai, live-aboard **dive cruises**, luxury **hotel boats** on the Nile and escorted sightseeing tours of the main **archaeological sites**. For details of tour operators specializing in tours to Egypt, see Travel Tips (page 122).

Below: *Red Sea corals are among the marine attractions for divers visiting the Sinai Peninsula.*

Nuweiba

About 90km (60 miles) north of Dahab on the Gulf of Aqaba. Like Sharm el-Sheikh, Nuweiba has become the focal point of an extended development of hotels, resorts, and shops. It is also a major **commercial port**, with ferry and freight services across the Gulf to Aqaba in Jordan. The main commercial part of town is around the port, with most of the places to stay and eat in what is known locally as 'Nuweiba City' – the original settlement, most of which dates from the Israeli occupation years, 10km (6 miles) to the north of the harbour. Just 1km (0.5 mile) further north, on the same bay, a secondary development at **Tarabin** will one day merge with Nuweiba. Its sandy beach is popular with holidaying Israelis. Nuweiba lacks Dahab's laid-back charm, but makes up for it with good beaches and an awesome backdrop of savage red and gold mountains which are in sharp contrast to the blue waters of the Gulf of Aqaba.

Basata Village **

About 23km (14 miles) north of Nuweiba, in the region known as **Ras el-Burqa** on the Gulf of Aqaba, this purpose-built tourism settlement will appeal to anyone who finds Nuweiba over-commercialized. Inspired by the simple lifestyle of the **Bedouin**, the village offers bamboo huts for a shifting community of up to 150 visitors. You can also camp here for a nominal fee. Basata is a good base for exploring the trackless hinterland, with a variety of trips available by four-wheel-drive vehicle or by camel.

Taba

This resort settlement right on the Israeli border had the distinction of being the last piece of Egyptian territory to be handed back by Israel following the Camp David peace agreement between the two countries. It was the subject of pointless squabbling until 1989, when after arbitration Israel finally yielded. Its main function now is as the main **border crossing** between Sinai and Israel, with the popular Israeli beach resort of **Eilat** and the Jordanian port of **Aqaba** both within sight. There is a large luxury hotel, built when Taba looked set to remain Israeli and become a suburb of Eilat, and a small town centre inland from the tiny beach. There are plans for an airport at Taba, but until it is built this tiny border town is likely to retain its out-of-the-way ambience.

Satellite Launch

Egypt became the first country in the Arab and African world to join the space age in April 1998, with the launch of **Nilesat 101**, a sophisticated communications satellite. A second satellite, **Nilesat 102**, was launched from the European Space Agency's base at **Korou**, French Guiana, in August 2000.

Geziret Phara'un (Pharaoh's Island) **

Situated 8km (5 miles) south of Taba. A **Crusader castle**, captured by **Saladin** in 1170, is one of the attractions of this tiny offshore islet. It has been rebuilt so many times that it resembles a modern bunker more than a medieval fortress, but the day trip to the island is pleasant and there is good snorkelling and diving from its shores. Open 09:00–17:00.

'The Fjord' *

Located approximately 15km (10 miles) south of Taba. This local beauty spot has dramatic cliffs and a relatively undeveloped beach, but little else to recommend it.

Opposite top: *Bedouin nomads wander the Sinai Peninsula, setting up camp wherever they find grazing for their flocks.*

Below: *Ramparts of the Crusader fortress at Geziret Phara'un.*

Sinai at a Glance

Best Times to Visit

Year-round, but some may find the intense heat of June–September in Sinai oppressive. December–March the sun shines but the water is too cold for pleasurable swimming.

Getting There

The Eastern Desert

Direct **charter flights** to Hurghada from UK and Europe. **Internal flights** to Luxor, Cairo, Alexandria. **Highway 44** connects Hurghada and Safaga with Suez; direct **express buses** operate between Cairo and Hurghada. At Safaga, the highway turns to connect the coast with the Nile Valley at Qena. There are no rail services. El-Gouna is 20 minutes by **taxi** or **limousine** transfer from Hurghada Airport. Travel **by road** from Luxor via Qena/Safaga/Hurghada; from Cairo via Zafrana.

The Canal Towns

Flights to Port Said and Suez from Cairo and Alexandria. **Main roads** and **express bus routes** connect Cairo with Suez, Ismailia and Port Said. Express buses travel on from Suez to Sharm el-Sheikh, Nuweiba and Eilat in Israel. A **coastal highway** runs along the western shore of the Gulf to Hurghada and Safaga. A **rail route** runs via Zagazig to Ismailia and another from Cairo to Suez. A railway runs parallel to the Canal, connecting Port Said, Ismailia and Suez.

Sinai

Express buses from Cairo via Suez cross under the Canal and follow Highway 66 round to Sharm el-Sheikh and beyond. **Flights** by EgyptAir and other charter airlines direct into Sharm el-Sheikh. Also domestic flights from Cairo, Luxor, Alexandria. Fast **catamaran ferries** operate between Hurghada and Sharm el-Sheikh. There are no rail services.

Getting Around

Minibuses and **taxis** are the normal public transport in the Sinai and Red Sea resorts. In El-Gouna take taxis or **electric golf carts**, or travel on foot. In Port Said and Ismailia, **horse-drawn carriages** called *hantours* are a more picturesque option; haggle to set a price before starting your journey.

Where to Stay

Hurghada

Luxury

Hurghada Inter-Continental Resort & Casino, PO Box 36, Hurghada, tel: (065) 446-911, fax: (065) 446-910. Choice of restaurants, parasailing, windsurfing, dive centre, tennis.

Mid-Range

Grand Hotel Hurghada, Cornish Road, Hurghada, tel: (065) 443-751, fax: (065) 443-750. Gardens, private beach, dive centre, terrace bars and three restaurants.

Budget

Panorama Hotel, El-Dahar, Hurghada, tel and fax: (065) 548-890. Cheap, central location, basic.

El-Gouna

For all information and reservations, El-Gouna, 26 July St, Agouza, Cairo, tel: (02) 305-7843, fax: (02) 302-3201, e-mail: info@elgouna.com

Luxury

Sheraton Miramar Resort. Five-star mega-resort with 282 rooms, two restaurants, five pools, aquacentre, dive centre, health club, shopping arcade.

El-Khan. 25 rooms, three stars, this boutique inn is as close to budget accommodation as El-Gouna gets. Recommended.

Port Said

Luxury

Sonesta Hotel, Sharia Filastin, tel: (066) 325-511, fax: (066) 324-825. Five-star hotel with excellent views.

Helnan Port Said Hotel, New Cornish, tel: (066) 320-890, fax: (066) 323-762. Five-star on the beach.

Sharm el-Sheikh

Best choice of hotels is not in Sharm itself but at its annex, Na'ama Bay, where most streets are unnamed.

Luxury

Hilton al-Fayrouz Village, Na'ama Bay, tel: (069) 600-136, fax: (069) 601-043. Village-style luxury resort in landscaped grounds.

Sinai at a Glance

Movenpick Hotel, Na'ama Bay, tel: (069) 600-100, fax: (069) 600-111. Enormous Swiss-run chain resort with excellent sports facilities.
Sonesta Beach Resort, Na'ama Bay, tel: (069) 600-725, fax: (069) 600-733. Luxury five-star complex with pools, bars and restaurants.

Mid-Range

Ghazala Hotel, Na'ama Bay, tel: (069) 600-150, fax: (069) 600-155. Attractive, affordable bungalow complex just inland from the pedestrian beachfront esplanade.

Budget

Hotel Sanafir, Na'ama Bay, tel: (069) 600-197, fax: (069) 600-196. Close to the beach.

Dahab

Accommodation is very basic, with Bedouin-run campsites offering bamboo huts or concrete shacks with communal toilets and showers. These are only really suitable for backpackers on a tight budget. There are no luxury hotels.

Where to Eat

In all the Sinai and Red Sea resorts except Hurghada the choice is between **hotel restaurants** (all hotels listed have adequate restaurants) and nameless eating places in local **bazaars** or on the beach. Hurghada's cosmopolitan clientele ensures there are restaurants serving food from all over the world. Most restaurants have no fax numbers.

Hurghada

Portofino, General Hospital Street, El-Dahar, Hurghada, tel: (065) 546-250, no fax. Italian and seafood specialities.
Lagoona Restaurant, Hurghada Hilton Resort, tel: (065) 442-113 Expensive fish.
Chez Dominique Restaurant, Sonesta Beach Resort, tel: (065) 443-660. Fine French cooking.
Felfela, Sheraton Road, tel: (065) 442-410, fax: (065) 442-411.
Nawara, Hurghada Touristic Centre, tel: (065) 446-053. Lebanese and Egyptian.

Tours and Excursions

Hurghada

Aquascope, reservation desks at all main hotels in Hurghada, tel and fax: (065) 446-906. Submarine trips round offshore islands. Most have their own dive centre; also dive centres in the town.

Sinai

Tour desks in all major **hotels** offer **excursions** to Mt Sinai, St Catherine's, the Coloured Canyon, Pharaoh's Island. Most major hotels also have resident dive shops offering escorted **dive trips** to the Ras Mohammed Marine National Park and dive sites throughout the region. **SIAG Desert Tours**, Hurghada, tel: (065) 443-240; Sharm el-Sheikh, tel: (069) 600-860. Four-wheel-drive **desert safaris**, diving trips. **Balloons over Egypt**, 11th Floor, Nile Tower, 21 Sharia Giza, Cairo, tel: (02) 332-3751, fax: (02) 332-3761. Balloon flights over St Catherine's monastery and Mt Sinai, **quad bike trips** into desert. **Dive companies** based at almost every hotel in all Sinai resorts. Ensure that your company complies with international standards set by PADI or other reputable dive organizations.

Useful Contacts

There are tourist information offices only in Hurghada and Sharm el-Sheikh. Neither offers much local information.

Hurghada

Tourist Office, Bank Misr Street, tel: (065) 444-420.

Sharm el-Sheikh

Tourist Office, Port Authority Building, tel: (069) 600-170.
Red Sea Bulletin, PO Box 191, Hurghada, tel: (065) 446-462, is an amateurish but useful guide to activities, nightlife and places to eat.

SINAI & RED SEA	J	F	M	A	M	J	J	A	S	O	N	D
AVERAGE TEMP. °F	61	68	66	71	79	84	86	87	83	77	70	65
AVERAGE TEMP. °C	16	20	19	21.5	26	29	30	30.5	28.5	25	21	18
HOURS OF SUN DAILY	11	11	11	11	12	12	12	12	12	11	11	11
RAINFALL	0	0	0	0	0	0	0	0	0	0	0	0

8
Western Desert Oases

West of the Nile the Western Desert rolls away towards **Libya**. Uninhabited and all but uninhabitable, it is punctuated by a handful of oases where water welling up from deep below the surface irrigates gardens of date palms. These pockets of fertility can be quite large – **Dakhla**, the largest true oasis, covers more than 1000 sq km (386 sq miles) – and provide a living for thousands of villagers. Until recently, these were the least-visited communities, but the construction of a 1000km (621-mile) road loop connecting them with Cairo and the Nile has brought greater contact with tourism. Some oases have a few ancient temples and tombs to show that they may in ancient times have been less isolated.

To leave the rich, cultivated fields and plantations of the **Nile Valley** for the empty dunes and saltpans of the **Western Desert** is to enter a different world, inhabited by only a tiny handful of Egypt's people: wandering **Bedouin** finding pasture for their goats and sheep in the seemingly inhospitable landscape, and hardy **oasis-dwellers** eking out a living in isolation from the rest of the world in fertile pockets where date palms cluster around lakes fed by underground aquifers. The harsh existence of the nomad and the comparatively luxurious life of the oasis villager occasionally clashed in the past, when desert raiders attacked oasis settlements. Today, both are encountering the outside world in force for the first time, with airfields and desert highways, projects to irrigate the desert, and efforts by the Egyptian government to force the Bedouin into permanent settlements.

DON'T MISS

*** **Dakhla:** largest of the oases with medieval citadel and villages, ancient tombs and temples.
*** **Siwa:** most remote and most exotic oasis, with temples, hot springs and a unique culture.
** **Baharia:** colourful, old-fashioned villages and markets.
* **Farafra:** smallest and least visited of the oases.

Opposite: *Iceberg-like rock formations in the White Desert region.*

Above: *Donkeys are the favoured form of transport for oasis farmers.*
Opposite: *Islands of fertile greenery are surrounded by desert sands.*

Western Desert Oases

Kharga ★

About 240km (150 miles) west of Asyut, Kharga is the most accessible and the least spectacular oasis. It is the heart of the **New Valley Project**: since the 1950s, hundreds of wells have been bored into the aquifer, irrigating great areas of land. Population pressure in Egypt is huge, but the Kharga project has been more a matter of national prestige than an attempt to address the population problem, as the new homes and farmland it can provide are negligible compared with population growth. El-Kharga, the capital of the region, is a modern town of 65,000 people and is the transport and accommodation hub for the oasis.

The **Temple of Hibis,** 2km (1 mile) north of the town, is a small 6th-century BC temple to Amun. It is closed for restoration, and the site is unenclosed. Visible from the road, the **Temple of Nadura** is 1.5km (0.75 mile) north of town. It is also unenclosed, but the watchman expects baksheesh. This much ruined small temple dates from the **Roman era** and is worth visiting for its desert views.

Dakhla ★★

Some 190km (115 miles) west of Kharga, this is the largest true oasis (not counting Faiyum, which is an extension of the Nile Valley), and covers 1125 sq km (434 sq miles). Twelve small villages are scattered around the oasis, which is watered by hundreds of springs and pools. The largest settlement is **Mut**. Between Sharia el-Wadi and Sharia el-Basatin in Mut is the unenclosed **Citadel and Old City**. Crumbling mud walls enclose a low hilltop surrounded by a maze of roofless mud-brick houses and lanes.

El-Qasr is 35km (22 miles) north of Mut. A step back into the Middle Ages, this village is a place of narrow lanes and mud-brick houses with a 12th-century **mosque**.

Western Desert Oases Climate

As can be expected, the Western Desert has an extreme desert climate. It becomes very hot during the day year-round, although it can be quite chilly at night. Avoid May–September. This area is best visited in **winter**.

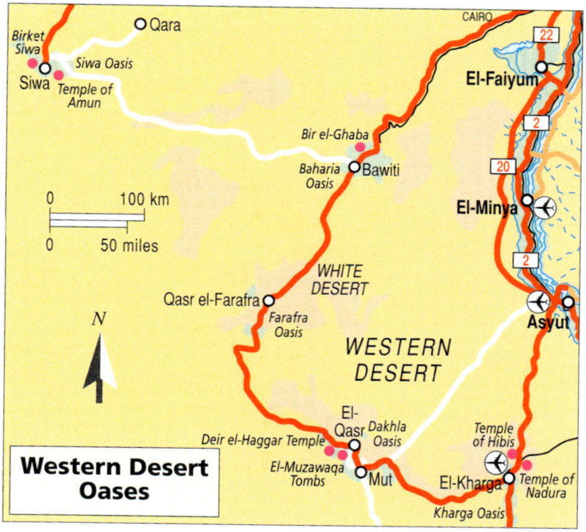

Just 5km (3 miles) west of El-Qasr are the **El-Muzawaqa** tombs from the **Middle Kingdom** era. Two main tombs are decorated with frescoes; others are just pits in the hillside. **Deir el-Haggar Temple** is 8km (5 miles) west of El-Qasr. This 1st-century AD temple was recently excavated and rebuilt. Open 09:00–16:00.

New light has been cast on Dakhla with the discovery by Canadian archaeologists of Roman and Pharaonic **monuments** at a site called **Asmant el-Kharab**. They include the remains of a town of two-storeyed mud-brick houses from the 4th century AD, grouped around the ruins of a temple built during the reign of Nero to the demigod Toter. Engraved stone tombs were found too. (Not open to visitors.)

Temple on the Move

Archaeologists in 1998 warned of the need to move the **Temple of Hibis** in Kharga Oasis to a site 500m (550yd) north of its original location, where ground water threatens to destroy the fragile monument. The temple is relatively well preserved from the Third Pylon onwards, and the ornamentation inside consists mainly of animals.

Baharia **

Baharia Oasis, 340km (211 miles) southwest of Cairo, is home to 10,000 villagers in four small villages and is noted for its **hot springs**. Just outside the main village of **Bawiti** is the **Valley of the Golden Mummies**, the extensive Graeco-Roman necropolis discovered in 1998. About 20km (12 miles) east of Bawiti village, **Bir el-Ghaba** has **natural hot springs** among the palm trees.

Farafra *

Some 180km (110 miles) west of Baharia, this is the most primitive oasis, with one small settlement (called **Qasr el-Farafra**). The oasis is best known for the wind-sculpted limestone formations of the nearby **White Desert**.

ALEXANDER AT SIWA

Hearing of the **oracle of Amun at Siwa** following his conquest of Egypt, Alexander the Great marched across the desert from the coast. The megalomaniac Macedonian hoped the oracle would confirm his conviction that he was the son of **Zeus** – confirmation that the priests of Amun sensibly gave. More pragmatically, Alexander also sought and gained confirmation that he was the son of **Amun** and the rightful Pharaoh. Alexander and the Ptolemies who succeeded him saw no contradiction between the Egyptian pantheon and their own gods, indentifying Amun with Zeus and finding Egyptian identities for their other deities.

SIWA

Until recently Siwa, approximately 840km (525 miles) west of Cairo, 300km (180 miles) southwest of Mersa Matruh, and quite close to the border with Libya, was closed to visitors for security reasons as it had a large military base. Siwa is a unique desert enclave, with its own peculiar **traditions** (women are always veiled in the *tarfadit*, a blue cotton robe, and married women are not allowed to speak to any men outside their family circle) and also its own **language**, a dialect of Berber. The people of Siwa are descended from **Berber** tribes who may have settled here as long as 2000 years ago, and the first Europeans to visit the area arrived only after Napoleon's invasion of Egypt. With few facilities for visitors, it is a haven for those who want to get off the beaten track. The oasis is 12m (40ft) below sea level, and is almost unbelievably lush, producing not only **dates** but **olives** and **grain**. Siwa has one main settlement, with a variety of sights scattered around the area.

Below: *The mud-brick battlements of Shali Citadel overlook Siwa town in the heart of the oasis.*

Shali Citadel ★★

Centre of Siwa, unenclosed. The mud-brick battlements of this **medieval fort** surround a **mosque** and the only chimney shaped **minaret** in Egypt.

Temple of Amun ★

Just 4km (2.5 miles) east of town, the Temple of Amun is unenclosed. It is the main attraction in Siwa. Built in the 7th century BC, the temple was noted in ancient times for its **oracle**, and **Alexander the Great** came here to consult it. The temple is in ruins.

Geziret Fatnas ('Fantasy Island')

About 6km (3.5 miles) west of town. Natural bathing pool on an island covered with tropical greenery and set in the salty **Birket**, or Lake, **Siwa**.

Western Desert Oases at a Glance

Best Times To Visit

In **November–March** the days are hot and sunny. Nights in the desert can be chilly (even close to zero in high country in winter). Daytime temperatures from April–October are almost intolerable; few if any buildings have air conditioning.

Getting There

The only scheduled **EgyptAir** flights are between Cairo, Kharga and Dakhla (listed in timetables as 'New Valley'). Air services to Siwa are irregular. **Buses** to Kharga and Dakhla from Cairo and Asyut. Buses to Siwa from Mersa Matruh. **Shared taxis** also operate.

Getting Around

The best way to see the oases is on an **organized tour**. Public transport is erratic and accommodation can be hard to find. Independent travel here is only for the bold.
Minibuses, taxis and **shared taxis** operate in and among villages and between oases.

Where to Stay

Accommodation is limited as the oases have only recently opened for tourism and still see few visitors; there is no luxury accommodation and very few mid-range hotels.

El-Kharga
Mid-Range
El-Kharga Oasis Hotel, Midan Nasser, tel: (092) 921-500. Modern, comfortable hotel with 35 rooms and garden restaurant.

Dakhla
Budget
Mebarez Hotel, Sharia el-Qasr, Mut, tel: (092) 821-524, no fax. Cheap, some rooms with bath, decent restaurant.

Baharia
Mid-Range
International Hot Springs Hotel, Bawiti, tel: (012) 321-2179. Modern rooms around garden, hot spring pool.

Siwa
Budget
Arous el-Waha Hotel, tel: (046) 460-2100. Rooms with fan and constant hot water.

Farafra
Mid-Range
El-Badawiya Hotel, tel: (012) 214-8343. Comfortable, attractive hotel, arranges White Desert safaris.

Where to Eat

All the **listed hotels** have acceptable restaurants serving Egyptian and western food. Alternatives include simple fuul and felafel stands and restaurants in main villages.

Tours and Excursions

Trips to the Siwa Oasis can be arranged from Alexandria by contacting travel agencies including:
Misr Hanoville, 19 Sharia Sa'ad Zaghloul, tel: (03) 486-6501, no fax.
Misr Travel, 33 Salah Salim, tel and fax: (02) 684-6971.
Thomas Cook, 15 Sharia Sa'ad Zaghloul, tel: (03) 487-5118, fax: (03) 487-4073.
Chauffeur-driven cars can be rented by the day or week from **Limousine Rent Cars**, 25 Talaat Harb, tel: (03) 486-5253.
Visits to other oases, excursions and desert safaris are best arranged from Cairo with tour agencies including: **Min Travel**, 15A Ain Shams Street, El-Naam, Cairo, tel: (02) 637-9961, fax: (02) 761-7165.
Isis Travel, 48 El-Giza Street, Orman Building, Giza, Cairo, tel: (02) 749-4322, fax: (02) 748-4821.

Useful Contacts

El-Kharga
Tourist Office, Midan Nasser, tel and fax: (092) 921-206.

Dakhla
Tourist Office, tel: (092) 821-686, no fax. Information, maps, trips around the oasis.

OASES	J	F	M	A	M	J	J	A	S	O	N	D
AVERAGE TEMP. °F	57	61	66	72	83	86	89	86	84	75	66	61
AVERAGE TEMP. °C	14	16	19	22	28.5	30	31.5	30	29	24	19	16
HOURS OF SUN DAILY	6	7	8	9	11	12	12	12	11	11	10	8
RAINFALL	0	0	0	0	0	0	0	0	0	0	0	0

Travel Tips

Tourist Information

The Egyptian Tourist Authority has offices in London, New York, San Francisco, Chicago, Johannesburg and Montreal. Head Office: Misr Travel Tower, Abbassia Square, Cairo, tel: (02) 285-3576, fax: (02) 285-4363.
Local tourist offices can be found in Cairo, Port Said, Alexandria, Suez, Aswan, Luxor, Hurghada and Sharm el-Sheikh.A comprehensive list of tour operators specializing in tours to Egypt is available from Egyptian Tourist Authority Offices overseas (*see above*) and from the Association of Independent Tour Operators in the UK, 133A St Margaret's Road, Twickenham, Middlesex TW1 1RG, tel: (020) 8744-9280, fax: (020) 8744-3187.
Specialist operators include:
Desert and oasis safaris
Exodus Travels, 9 Weir Road, London SW12 0LT, tel: (020) 8675-5550, fax: (020) 8673-0779, e-mail: sales@exodustravels.co.uk, website: www.exodustravels.co.uk
Explore Worldwide, 1 Frederick Street, Aldershot. Hampshire GU11 1LQ, tel: (01252) 760-000, fax: (01252) 760-001, e-mail: info@explore.co.uk, website: www.explore.co.uk
Battlefield tours
Holts' Tours, Golden Key Building, 15 Market Street, Sandwich, Kent CT13 9DA, tel: (01304) 612-248, fax: (01304) 614-930, website: www.battletours.co.uk

Entry Requirements

All visitors require a national passport with at least six months' validity. All foreign visitors require visas, obtainable on arrival or in advance from your nearest Egyptian consulate. Visas are valid for a month, and you will not be allowed to leave Egypt with an out-of-date visa.

Customs

Duty free allowances are: 1 litre/1 quart spirits, 1 litre/1 quart perfume, 200 cigarettes and 25 cigars. Duty free is available on arrival at international airports. Travellers with video cameras or laptop computers may be required to fill in a form on arrival, guaranteeing that they will re-export them on departure.

Health Requirements

Proof of immunization against cholera and yellow fever is required for those arriving from infected areas, including southern Africa and South America. No other immunizations are mandatory.

Getting There

By air: There are direct flights to Cairo from all of the European capitals and other major cities, and from the USA, Canada, Australia, most African states, and all Middle Eastern capitals. Some international flights also connect Alexandria and Luxor with European cities.
Charter flights operate from the UK and Europe directly into regional airports including Luxor, Hurghada and Sharm el-Sheikh. These are sold as part of a package holiday including accommodation.
By road: Express coach services connect Cairo via Suez

and Sinai with Eilat in Israel. Foreigners may not use the border with Sudan.
By rail: No international rail services.
By ferry: Limited services from Greek ports including Piraeus (Athens) and Heraklion (Crete).

What to Pack

Egypt is a conservative Muslim society. Shorts, T-shirts and beachwear are acceptable only in resorts on the Red Sea which receive many European tourists, and even then only on the beach. Elsewhere, revealing garments are frowned on and in the case of women they will definitely encourage harassment. Light long-sleeved shirts or blouses, long trousers and frocks will not offend local sensibilities and are also a sensible precaution against the powerful sun. Women may be required to wear a headscarf in religious buildings. In winter, nights can be chilly even in Upper Egypt. Pack a medium-weight sweater or jacket. Mosquito repellent containing 'deet' (diethyltoluamide) is best. Photographers using slide or specialist film should take a plentiful supply as only standard film is usually available locally. Sunglasses protect eyes against fierce sun, dust and urban air pollution.

Money Matters

The Egyptian pound is divided into 100 piastres. Egyptian currency is not obtainable abroad. US dollars, sterling and euros are readily exchangeable at banks and hotels. Small-denomination notes and coins are useful in view of demands for 'baksheesh' (tips) from guides, porters, boatmen, taxi and carriage drivers, gatekeepers and beggars. The best way to carry money is in travellers' cheques in smaller denominations (e.g. UK£20 or US$50) to avoid carrying a lot of cash at any time. Banks normally offer a better rate of exchange, or charge less commission, than hotel desks or money-changers. Do not be tempted by offers to exchange money on the black market which in practice no longer exists; such offers are scams. Credit cards are accepted in larger hotels, restaurants and shops in Cairo and the main tourist areas, but not really elsewhere. ATMs accepting Visa, Master and Cirrus cards are now widely available.

Accommodation

Hotels are graded from five-star deluxe to one-star by the Egyptian Tourist Authority. In the two major cities and the main tourist centres, accommodation ranges from five-star hotels operated by major international chains to cheap hotels catering to ordinary Egyptians. The cheapest ones (which generally escape the rating system entirely) are very basic, with only rudimentary facilities, and may be unacceptably dirty; they will appeal only to the most tightfisted budget traveller. Anything below three-star grading is unlikely to offer the tourist a very pleasant stay.

Public Holidays

25 April • Sinai Liberation Day
1 May • May Day
23 July • Revolution Day
6 October • National Day
For religious holidays and festivals, see page 126.

Eating Out

Cairo and Alexandria have some excellent Egyptian and international restaurants, many within major hotels. Hurghada and Sharm el-Sheikh, both of which attract package holidaymakers, abound in generic European, German, Italian, Scandinavian and (in Hurghada) even Russian eating places. Elsewhere, the choice is between hotel restaurants and simple street stands and eating places, often nameless, where there is no written menu and the dish of the day is likely to be one of the local staples. The price range is equally wide.

Transport

By air: EgyptAir flies from Cairo to regional airports including Alexandria, Sharm el-Sheikh, Luxor, Hurghada, Aswan, Abu Simbel and Suez.
By road: An international driving licence is required. Avoid renting from local car hire agencies as deals offered by international chains are equally cheap and vehicles and paperwork more reliable. You should always carry your licence and all vehicle papers at all times as they must be produced at police checkpoints. Take out maximum

insurance, including collision damage waiver, as the risk of an accident is high. Drive defensively as other vehicles are usually driven recklessly and at high speed. The official speed limit is 90 kph (55 mph) on ordinary highways and 100 kph (64 mph) on four-lane motorways but this limit is generally ignored. Do not drive at night unless absolutely necessary. Drive on the right, but be aware that off main highways (and even on them) signposting hardly exists and is usually in Arabic. Off-road drivers in Sinai and the Western Desert beware of mines left after WWII or the Arab-Israeli wars. Cars with a driver can also be rented.

By bus: Long-distance buses operate on all the intercity routes and range from air-conditioned express coaches to slow, elderly vehicles which make frequent stops. Fares are cheap, and express buses are sometimes faster than trains.You cannot book tickets or obtain timetable information by telephone; if you are in a cheap hotel frequented by budget travellers, you may be able to buy tickets at the hotel. Otherwise arrange transport in person at the bus station. Tight security aga nst terrorism means plainclothes policemen ride shotgun on many intercity buses. On some routes, tourists are required to travel on special services in convoy.

Shared Taxis: Between towns and villages, many Egyptians travel by shared taxis which travel a set route and depart when full ... very full. Taxi travel is hair-raising, but in some areas it may be the only option. Shared taxis usually congregate at stands close to main local bus or rail stations.

By trains: Egypt's main railway lines are from Cairo south to Aswan, via Luxor and the Nile Valley, and north to Alexandria through the Delta. They also run from Cairo direct to Suez and between Suez and Port Said, paralleling the Canal. First class is comfortable, second class reasonable, third class only for the desperate. Reservations and information are not available by telephone, and often impossible in person. Book rail tickets through your hotel or local travel agency, at least three days in advance.

Cairo: Ramses Station, Midan Ramses, open 24 hours. First, second and third class trains to all destinations; Wagons-Lits sleeping cars to Luxor and Aswan. For berths, tel and fax: (02) 795-2966.

Alexandria: Masr Station, Sharia Muharram Bey, open 24 hours.

Luxor: Luxor Station, Midan el-Mahatta, open 24 hours.

Aswan: Only three services (a sleeper and two express trains) per day for foreigners travelling between Cairo and Aswan.

For local transport, Cairo and Alexandria have municipal bus services and only Cairo has a metro system. Elsewhere, minibuses are the main form of transport. Taxis are cheap and the best way of getting around. Open-topped horse-drawn carriages (caleches or hantours) ply the corniches of Luxor, Alexandria and Port Said. Negotiate a price before boarding.

By boat: Many river cruisers or 'floating hotels' operate on the Nile. There are currently no cruises between Cairo and Luxor but cruises do operate between Luxor and Aswan in each direction and are included in the brochures of most international tour operators to Egypt. It is cheaper to hire a

Road Signs

Road signs are often bilingual in Arabic and English but are very few and far between even in major tourist areas, and virtually nonexistent off the main highways.

Conversion Chart

From	To	Multiply By
Millimetres	Inches	0.0394
Metres	Yards	1.0936
Metres	Feet	3.281
Kilometres	Miles	0.6214
Square kilometres	Square miles	0.386
Hectares	Acres	2.471
Litres	Pints	1.760
Kilograms	Pounds	2.205
Tonnes	Tons	0.984

To convert Celsius to Fahrenheit: x 9 ÷ 5 + 32

USEFUL PHRASES

Hello • salaam aleikum
Hello (response) • aleikum es-salaam
How are you? • izzayak (m), izzayik (f)
Where is? • feyn?
Station • mahatta
Hotel • funduk
Toilet • twalet
How much? • bekaam?
Too much • da ghaali awi
Go away! • Imshi!
(*see* also page 110)

felucca (traditional sailing boat) and crew from Aswan to Luxor; strike a deal on the Aswan waterfront or arrange through an Aswan travel agency (*see* Aswan At a Glance, page 101).
Liveaboard Dive Cruises: fully inclusive dive cruises from Red Sea ports including Sharm el-Sheikh and Hurghada.

Business Hours
Government offices 09:00–14:00,most closed Thursdays and Fridays. Banks and commercial offices: 08:30–13:30, most closed on Fridays, some on Sundays.

Time Difference
GMT +2; in summer GMT+3.

Communications
Central Post Office, Midan el-Ataba, Cairo, open 24 hours. Other post offices open 08:30–15:00, closed Friday. It is much easier to post letters and postcards from your hotel, which will sell stamps. Letters weighing less than 100g (4 oz) can be sent by premium rate Express Mail. Telephones are available in most hotels, and metered telephones in cafés and restaurants. There is normally a substantial minimum charge for international calls from hotels and prices may be heavily loaded. In Cairo you can also make international calls from the PTT offices at Midan el-Tahrir, Sharia Alfi Bey and Sharia Adly, all open 24 hours. Fax services are also available from hotels and at PTT offices. Street payphones have recently become widespread. International dialling codes from Egypt are:
UK (00 44); USA and Canada (00 1); Australia (00 61); New Zealand (00 64); South Africa (00 67); Ireland (00 353).
Enquiries tel: 140.

Electricity
220V AC; sockets take European-style two pin plug.

Weights and Measures
Metric system is used.

Health Precautions
Seek medical advice regarding immunizations, including those against meningitis, hepatitis, polio, tetanus, typhoid and diphtheria. Tap water should not be trusted, even in Cairo. Bottled water is available. Bilharzia, an infestation carried by water snails, is prevalent in Egypt and can damage internal organs. Do not swim in the Nile or Lake Nasser at any point, and seek medical treatment if you do happen to fall in.
Be especially aware of sunburn: the Egyptian sun burns even in winter. Use high-factor sun block when sailing, snorkelling, engaging in watersports, or sunbathing. Wear a hat at archeological sites, where there is little shade. Especially in summer, drink plenty of water – you may not feel yourself sweating, but the dry air dehydrates your body very quickly.

Health Services
Public health services are limited and good private hospitals are only found in Cairo. Make sure you have adequate insurance to cover the cost of private health care in case of accident or illness, including medical repatriation expenses.

NUMBERS

0 • sifr
1 • wahid
2 • itnayn
3 • talaata
4 • arbah
5 • khamsa
6 • sitta
7 • sabah
8 • tamanya
9 • tesah
10 • ashara
11 • hidashar
12 • itnashar
13 • talatashar
14 • arbatashar
15 • khamastashar
16 • sittashar
17 • sabahtashar
19 • tisatashar
20 • ishrin
21 • wahid wi'ishrin
30 • talatin
40 • arba'in
50 • khamsin
60 • sittin
70 • sab'in
80 • tamanin
90 • tis'in
100 • miyya
500 • khumsu miyya
1000 • alf

Personal Safety

Between 1992 and 1997 extremists conducted a campaign of violence against the government.In 1997 ten German tourists were killed in Cairo and gunmen killed 58 tourists in Luxor. Since then security has been stepped up, but visitors are advised to be vigilant and respect advice from security authorities. Terrorism aside, violent crime against visitors is rare, though theft and pickpocketing are rife. Watch your belongings at all times, use hotel safes if available, and keep travellers cheques, money and tickets on your person in a concealed wallet, inner pocket or money-belt. Be especially wary on city buses. Road accidents are frequent and windscreens may be smashed by flying pebbles. Avoid sitting in the front seat of taxis or minibuses and do not travel in these at night. Have nothing to do with drugs. The minimum sentence for bringing drugs into Egypt is 25 years in prison, and even the death sentence could be applicable to a drugs offence.

Emergencies

Cairo emergencies: Ambulance 123; Fire brigade 125; Police 122; Tourist Police 126. Do not count on any of these speaking English.

Etiquette

Wearing skimpy clothes away from Red Sea resorts will offend Egyptian sensibilities (*see* What to Pack). Remove shoes when entering a place of worship or a private home. Women may be asked to cover their heads inside a mosque or church. Egypt has a relaxed attitude to alcohol, but public drunkenness is strongly disapproved of. Public displays of affection between the sexes are taboo, though Egyptian men embrace on meeting and are often seen holding hands. Do not photograph people without permission, and do not take photographs of or near military installations.

Language

Arabic, in its Egyptian dialect, is the national language, but English is spoken in hotels and by shopkeepers and guides.

Holidays and Festivals

The Islamic calendar differs from the Western, with twelve lunar months and a year that is 11 days shorter, so holidays arrive 10–12 days earlier each year. As they depend on the first sighting of the new moon, dates cannot be predicted far in advance. Major events of the Egyptian year include:

Ramadan – the month of fasting, during which Muslims may not eat between sunrise and sunset; they tend to make up for this after dark. Most government offices have shorter working hours during Ramadan.

Eid el-Fitr – three-day celebration of the end of Ramadan, mainly a family festival, with new clothes for all and much eating. Avoid travel during Eid, when all Egypt is on the move.

Moulid el-Nabi (12th day of Rabei el-Awal) – Feast of the Prophet's Birthday, processions in Cairo and elsewhere.

Eid el-Adha (10th day of Zoul Higga) – culmination of pilgrimage (hadj) to Mecca. Public transport crowded by pilgrims.

Sham el-Nessim (mid April) – follows Coptic Easter (on different dates each year) and is a national holiday.

Apart from religious festivals, Egypt also has public holidays (*see* page 123).

Good Reading

Bob Brier, *The Murder of Tutankhamun: a 3000 year old murder mystery* (Weidenfeld and Nicholson, 1998).

Howard Carter, *The Tomb of Tutankhamun* (reprint Bodley Head, 1983). Carter's account of his discoveries.

Barry Carman, *The Bimbashi McPherson* (BBC Publications, 1981). Letters from one of Cairo's great characters.

Leonard Cottrell, *Land of the Pharaohs* (Brockhampton Press 1962).

Lawrence Durrell, *The Alexandria Quartet* (Faber & Faber 1962). Portrait of a vanished polyglot city, World War II.

Lawrence Durrell, *The Durrell-Miller Letters, 1935–1980* (Faber & Faber, 1988). Durrell's correspondence from wartime Alexandria and Cairo.

Stephen Howe, *Afrocentrism: Mythical Pasts and Imagined Homes* (Verso, 1998).

J. G. Landels, *Engineering in the Ancient World* (Constable Publishers, 1998).

Afaf Lutfi al-Sayyid Marsot, *Egypt in the reign of Muhammad Ali* (Cambridge University Press, 1984).

Anthony McDermott, *Egypt from Nasser to Mubarak: A flawed Revolution* (Croom Helm, 1988).

INDEX

Note: Numbers in **bold** indicate photographs